ISBN 978-1-332-16030-3
PIBN 10292776

1 MONTH OF
FREE
READING

at
www.ForgottenBooks.com

By purchasing this book you are eligible for one month membership to ForgottenBooks.com, giving you unlimited access to our entire collection of over 1,000,000 titles via our web site and mobile apps.

To claim your free month visit:
www.forgottenbooks.com/free292776

HISTORICAL SKETCHES

OF

BRIDGEWATER

Oneida County, New York

With Papers and Anecdotes Relating to Pioneers and Events

Compiled and Published by
ELEANOR LOUISE PORTER
Bridgewater, New York

OXFORD, NEW YORK
THE OXFORD TIMES PRINT
1914

FOREWORD

In presenting these pages I am conscious that many important facts may have been omitted and others appearing herein may not be complete, but the purpose has been to compile in one book many facts that would be lost if they were not preserved in some such form.

It is acknowledged that less has been written of the town of Bridgewater than any other town in the county as there has been no effort to collect interesting bits of history identified with the lives of the people and institutions growing out of its settlement covering more than one hundred years. Historic buildings and landmarks have passed away and their history with them. Prominent families, whose lives were impressed upon the town, are little heard of or known to this generation. Each succeeding year has made it more difficult to obtain information concerning the remote history of the town and, indeed, it is hard to learn much that will give a picture of the village of Bridgewater twenty to thirty years previous to the Civil War. Other periods seem to have passed and the records with them. However, here and there through some family tradition or manuscript, old letters and records, we get a glimpse of the past. Through the kind assistance of the friends of Bridgewater this book has been made possible and with grateful appreciation I acknowledge their help and consideration in making possible the preservation of these stories and historical facts.

Again I wish to emphasize that this volume must leave out many interesting facts and reminiscences of historical value because they could not be gathered in time to incorporate herein. It has seemed wise to publish what has already been gathered while there is an awakened interest in the matter and at a later period to publish an additional volume. I have the opportunity to have this work printed now at a cost that will not exceed the sale of a reasonable number of books and which if done under other conditions, where I could not personally supervise it, the cost would be prohibitive. But the greater reason for doing it now is that I have been engaged for years gathering the material and some good friends who have kindly given me data have passed away, and others have had little expectation of seeing a work of this kind realized. Then, too, the appearance of the first volume will do much to bring out other stories and historical facts. As it is my purpose to continue the work for an additional volume I solicit and will welcome any information and help from the friends of Bridgewater. While this work is acknowledged incomplete, it does, however, present glimpse of Bridgewater from the time of settlement until now.

ELEANOR LOUISE PORTER.

EARLY SETTLEMENT

Time rolls his ceaseless course. The race of yore
  Who danced our infancy upon their knee,
And told our marvelling boyhood legends store
  Of their strange ventures happed by land or sea,
How they are blotted from the things that be!
  How few, all weak and withered of their force,
Wait on the verge of dark eternity,
  Like stranded wrecks, the tide returning hoarse,
To sweep them from our sight! Time rolls his ceaseless course.
              —"Lady of the Lake."

It is a keen delight, when treading the familiar streets of one's native town and roaming the adjacent hills and woods, to paint an imaginary picture of primeval days—the long silent days when Nature reigned supreme and the wind led the great orchestral choirs; when the bird notes were the symphonies of the endless forest—the days when the eternal sunshine searched through the interlacing tree tops, filtering through the branches to make the lacework on the spaces below; when the moon's soft beams flooded the landscape with its golden glow, sprinkling the heaven-reared pines with the glory of the night, and the stars caroled their evening songs of glodness, declaring the glory of the heavens in praise to their Creator.

Such was the home of the Red Man, and, whether his piercing eye scanned these scenes so familiar to us, or whether his stealthy tread broke the silence of our forests we know very little, but as time went on these haunts were invaded by the pioneers who braved the hardships and toils of establishing a home in a wilderness and it is to these brave settlers, who cut and hewed their way into the heart of the forest, that we owe the foundation of our early settlement and civilization.

GEOGRAPHICAL AND GEOLOGICAL

The town of Bridgewater is located in the southeastern part of Oneida county and lies in a valley which traverses it from north to south and the town extends on the elevations of the valley on the east and west. This section was formerly known as Bridgewater Flats. The northern section of the flat is about one mile wide and this decreases gradually to the south, where it diminishes to half a mile in width. The northern part is somewhat stony and the southern and central portions contain a sandy soil. It is a remarkably fertile section and the farms are extensively cultivated. It is reported that when the state geologist visited this town several years ago he gave the opinion that there was no rock formation within 1000 feet of the surface and this has been partially proven in the fact that no rocks have been discovered in the deepest wells. One of the head streams of the Unadilla River rises in Paris and flows south through the town. Another branch rises in the northwestern part of the town and empties into the main stream near the south bounds of the town. Another small branch is formed from springs, and crosses two of the streets in the village. The head waters of the Unadilla are pure and are a favorite home of the speckled trout. Lime stone was formerly found in the northern part of the town where originally there was a quarry, which extended over three or four hundred acres. In this same section, but higher than the limestone strata, a small coal mine was discovered on the farm belonging to Peleg Babcock. It was merely a thin vein and nothing developed from it. According to geologists of that time the vein was considered out of place, "For, although vastly higher than the coal region in Pennsylvania, it is too low for coal in this section. In other words the dip of the coal beds in that state is such that it would rise much above any section in this county. In the same formation with this stray vein of coal iron pyrites are found, which are quite inflammable and burn like wood." The formation of the soil on the east and west sides of the valley is quite dissimilar. A little south of the limestone strata in the northern part of the town the side hills contain slate. Opposite this, on the west side of the valley, is slab. The soil is gravelly loam on the east hill, and clay appears on the west.

THE PIONEERS.

In March, 1789, two cousins, Jesse and Joel Ives, left their home in Connecticut and set out to make a new home in the wilderness. The country was practically a forest and the way was hard and devious, but the goal was ever ahead and nothing daunted the hardy pioneers in search of a new home. On and on they came, with their scanty provisions, stopping now and then to hew their way through the forest; compelled to halt at times for rest and refreshment, but eagerly proceeding on their way, at last arriving on the summit of the hill on the south-west that overlooks our little village. The snow was still on the ground and a rude shack was improvised for shelter. They decided to locate here and a suitable place was selected, twelve acres were cleared and a log house was erected. About two lears later Abner Ives, a younger brother of Jesse Ives, brought his family to this clearing and joined their fortunes with the others in the new land. (References to the early settlers and their descendants will be found on other pages of this volume.)

The trip was made from Connecticut on ox-sleds, but it is hard for the people of this generation to adequately picture in the imagination the wanderers on their journey, threading their way through the primeval forest, bringing all their earthly possessions with them. Their hearts were full of hope and courage. Something of the grim courage of the adventurons life in subduing the wilderness; the sense of achievement in making way for civilization; the intimate touch with nature in the hardships of their tasks gave them returns in happiness that has satisfied the pioneers of all ages. These people loved the wilds and were happy in their primitive pursuits.

In 1791 the original log house of Joel and Jesse Ives gave way to a more commodious frame dwelling. A frame barn was also erected. The kitchen of this frame house built by Jesse Ives was later remodelled and formed the front of a newer house which was occupied by his daughter, Miss Charlotte Ives, whose death occurred December 23, 1891. It was in the spring of 1789 that Thomas Brown built a log house on the present site of Bridgewater village and was the first settler there. A year previous, Joseph Farwell came to these scenes and made a clearing in the locality of the W. J. Scott and Edward McDermott farms. He was accompanied by Ephraim Waldo and they came from Mansfield, Conn., by way of Paris Hill and followed a blazed trail. The transportation facilities were two yokes of oxen and an ox sled. Upon their arrival they erected a crude shack from boughs and stakes with sidings of blankets, which constituted their home until summer time. Two of their number moved into more comfortable dwellings, while the others remained a year longer. Farwell's house was made of logs and this was his home until three years later when he erected a frame building.

The name of Farwell's Hill was undoubtedly lost sight of following the transfer of the settlement to the present village; but historically it is used to identify the place as one of the ancient landmarks. This Farwell's Hill settlement was located at the line of Madison and Oneida counties, half a mile south of the present village and consisted of a post-office, two stores, Masonic lodge, an ashery and a number of dwellings. The settlement thrived for a number of years until the completion of the Cherry Valley turnpike, which passed north of the hill. The business interests were transferred to the line of this new highway, where a new settlement sprang up and Farwell's Hill declined and passed into history.

OTHER SETTLERS

Stewart Bennett, a blacksmith, located on the well-known Kirkland farm, which he sold to Stephen Kirkland, who came from Saybrook, Connecticut, in July, 1816. This farm was located north of Bridgewater on what is known as the Gooseville road. He transformed the house into a new building. Rev. Samuel Kirkland, the founder of Hamilton College, and a noted Indian missionary, was a relative of this family. The dwelling was a small frame house and was long occupied by the two brothers, Asa P. and Nathaniel Kirkland. Garrett Scott, father of the late Mrs. Helen Williams, came to Bridgewater from Madison county, where he was born in 1799. His father and grandfather, Amos Scott, Sr. and Jr., were among the earlier settlers of that county.

Frederick Peirce, of Mansfield, Conn., came to Bridgewater in 1796 from Brookline, Vt., with a family named Gurley, with whom he lived for several years. Mr. Gurley settled on the place north of Bridgewater village, which was later owned by Cornelius Conklin, and now known as the John Atkinson farm. Most of the early roads in town were laid out by Frederick Peirce. His son, Nehemiah N. Peirce, was born in this town in 1818. He was several times supervisor of the town and in 1849 represented his district in Assembly. In 1843 he was appointed to the position of Colonel in the New York State militia, and by that title was generally known.

BRIDGEWATER—1830-1835

Relating to the early history of Bridgewater, North Bridgewater and Babcock Hill, there are preserved in the records of the late Gould H. Parkhurst of North Bridgewater several sketches covering the early life of these sections and containing the principal actors of the different periods of growth. These articles were written for local papers about 1883-1885 and give a graphic account of the business and local history of the time. They are so splendidly prepared that the sketches are given in full in order to preserve his style and work and to give credit to a man who gave his time and attention to saving records of history for future generations. The different headings will explain the dates when articles were written and the periods which they covered.

Bridgewater was then a busy and lively little business inland town, with several stage lines running at the four points of the compass, with heavy four-horse coaches, and whose proprietors were such as John Butterfield, Jabez DeWolf, Gideon Myers and others. Those heavy coaches were generally loaded to their fullest capacity with passengers, carrying the mail and running night and day. It was a nightly experience to hear the drivers tooting their stage horns to arouse hotel keepers and postmasters to be on hand and ready for duty at midnight hours. The most prominent merchants then in trade were Isaac Woodworth, on the corner where C. O. Biederman's harness, trunk and jewelry store is now conducted; Col. Curry in general merchandise and the manufacture of boots and shoes in the place where W. C. Marsh is now in trade; Rhodes and Robbins in the brick store on the corner where Shean's hotel is; James Haight's hat shop a little south of the Universalist church and hat store, which was burned down on the site of Dr. Whitford's residence about 1835 or 1836; Theo. Page was then the proprietor of the Hibbard House and it was known as the Stage House.   The hotel on the opposite corner was then kept by one Greenwood, but was afterward burned down, and a portion of the old academy moved there and converted into the hotel recently kept by Frank Shean.   Major Absalom Groves lived where the family of the late Samuel Langworthy now resides and carried on the tanning business where Zenas Eldred's cheese factory is, and run an ashery a little north of the residence of Mrs. Moses.   Esq. Lorain Blackman was engaged in the distilling business a few rods south of James Taft's Jerod Mathers conducted a blacksmith shop now used as a dwelling just south of Woodworth's wagon shop.   The old academy stood on the unoccupied space of ground a little east of Dr. Whitford's residence and the lower portion was occupied by Delos DeWolf till about 1844, when he erected the store now occupied by George Greenman.   Dr. John F. Trowbridge then resided where W. C. Marsh is and was at the time a very prominent practicing physician and surgeon, was twice elected to the Assembly, in 1831 and 1840.   Dr. Hall, who came earlier, settled at the Center, practiced his profession, farmed it, and was quite a politician and one of the main pillars in the church then located on the corner of W. H. Briggs' lot.   This church was the largest in structure of any house in town or near here; the society, too, was very large and about 1834 it divided, one portion going to Cassville and the other to the village, where each built a church.   Judge Ruger and Willard Crafts then expounded the law and Ezra Brown and John Southworth administered justice to the people.   Frederick Peirce, who resided at North Bridgewater, was then the only surveyor in town or vicinity and performed all the business in that line in town.   He surveyed every public highway then in town and made a record, which can be found and seen at the town clerk's office.   Esq. Levi Carpenter, who then resided at the Center, but who removed to the village about 1833, was a very prominent and successful pettifogger in justice courts, was commissioner of deeds for many years, and held the office of town clerk till age and infirmity compelled him to retire from active and public life. John T. Clark was another of Bridgewater's noted public men, having been elected State Engineer in 1853.   Later back, Delos DeWolf was elected County Clerk (1843), appointed commissioner for the new capitol at Albany in 1871, elected presidential elector in 1868.   William C. Ruger, son of John Ruger, was elected to the office of chief judge of the court of appeals in 1882. N. N. Peirce, whose former residence was at North Bridgewater, but has resided in the village for several years past, was elected to the assembly in 1849 and served in the seventy-second session, Hamilton Fish then being Governor, and Amos K. Hadley, speaker.   As to the literary young men, probably no town in the county of Oneida, according to its number of inhabitants, has graduated as many students in old Hamilton College, or turned out in the various departments as many talented young men, as Bridgewater.

NOTE—Present owners and occupants of places mentioned in the above sketch: C. O. Biederman's store, L. H. Belz barber shop; W. C. Marsh store, building occupied by W. H. Rowland and burned in September, 1913; Shean's hotel, Cottage Hotel; Zenas Eldred cheese factory, livery stables; Woodworth's wagon shop, present site of R. J. Wilkinson's residence; George Greenman's store, Rising Brothers.

HISTORIC SKETCH

The following letter, containing the early history of Bridgewater, was written to William Southworth and read by him at the Centennial of the town on the 4th of July, 1889. Mr. Southworth was a native of Bridgewater and was born September 22, 1823, the son of John and Harriet Southworth. He was educated in the schools in Bridgewater and Clinton and in later years served as Supervisor for several terms. On other pages will be found his history of the old Congregational church at the Center. Mr. Southworth died in Bridgewater February 26th, 1899.

JANESVILLE, WIS.,
Dec. 8, 1888.

Friend Southworth:—

In looking over the papers of my deceased father I found the enclosed letters, which were written by Seth Brown, of Beloit. Mr. Brown, like my father, was a former resident of Bridgewater, and was the elder by about twenty years. On his frequent and always welcome visits at my father's, he delighted in calling from the stores of a most retentive memory incidents relating to men and events in the early history of old Bridgewater. One day, when both were a little mellow, father asked him to pen his recollections of that town. A year later the first of these papers were received. I send them to you, hoping to incite you to gather from living lips details which may soon exist only as tradition.

Yours sincerely,
MAXIMUS HOAXER.

The demise at Bridgewater of my early friend, Ephraim Waldo, at the age of 89 years forcibly admonishes me that if I would comply with your request for reminiscences of Bridgewater, I must not delay, as my summons hence may issue soon.

In the office of the probate judge of Middlesex Co., Conn., in the 10th year of American independence, was filed an indenture binding Seth, son of Steadfast Brown, deceased, late a corporal in Company E, 4th Regiment of the Connecticut line, to Alexander Tackles of said county. Said Seth Brown to receive proper fool and clothing, to be taught reading, writing, and arithmetic, to receive a copy of God's word, a new suit of clothes and 5 pounds lawful money of Connecticut at the age of 21 years. In November, 1795, Mr. Tackles removed his goods and chattels, of which Seth was a part, to the Whitestown county. From Schenectady we poled up the Mohawk in a bateau. November 17th we arrived at the Little Falls. A canal, one mile long, half of it through solid rock with a lift of 44 feet by five locks, was opened for boats that day. Tuesday and Wednesday, November 17th and 18th, 116 boats were locked through. Tuesday night we tied up at German Flats, now the village of Herkimer, 13 miles below Fort Schuyler, now Utica. The town was settled in 1722 by German Palatines. In 1757 five hundred French Canadians and Indians, in command of Col. Bellestre, destroyed the settlement. They came by the way of Oswego river, Oneida Lake, Fish Creek, Fort Bull (destroyed in 1756) down the Mohawk, crossing the river a little above the village. Oneida Indians warned the Palatines of coming danger, fifteen days before the attack, again a week later, and a third time when the allies were at Fort Stanwix. The facetious citizens heeded not the warning. On the 12th of November the storm burst on the devoted place. About forty persons were killed. More than one hundred were taken prisoner. Sixty houses and many barns were burned. Several hundred each of horses, horned cattle, sheep, and swine were taken or destroyed. On the south bank of the Mohawk in Fort Kayuri were 350 men in garrison, yet the French and Indians, after remaining three days, retired with three or four wounded, none killed. April following, the allies attacked the place, killing and wounding thirty and losing fifteen of their party. September, 1778, three Tories and 115 Indians under Theyendanegea (Joseph Brandt), burned 63 houses, 57 barns, killed or captured 235 horses, 320 horned cattle, of which 93 were oxen. Two lives were lost. You may think this is digression, but age is garrulous and dwells much in the past.

There was no turnpike in those days, neither railroad nor canal. The route to Bridgewater was like a boy's jacket—a roundabout. Friday evening, tired but happy, we stopped at a log tavern kept by Ezra Parker, near the old house now owned by Mrs. Alexander Brown, about a mile south of Cassville. Here we made the acquaintance of one of the denizens, "a fat and greasy citizen.'' He entertained us hugely at supper, not where he ate, but where he was eaten—his name was "Bruin." Tuesday evening we worshipped our "Penates" in a wee log cabin with a roof of bark, a chimney of clay, and a floor laid by Dame Nature, and built on land purchased of Elisha and Roger W. Steele. It was the west end of the farm now owned by H. W. Hill. Subsequently Mr. Tackles sold to Abner Ives and Eldred Peck, and purchased on the flat, selling a few years later to Obadiah Thorne and Frederick Pierce. In December, Joel Blair bought of the Steele brothers the farm to the west of ours, now owned by Michael Walsh. The Steele brothers owned the farm north of ours, now owned by John Jennings. They had bought the "betterments" of John Thompson and Tim White. Elisha Steele left the town in 1806, but Roger W. retained the farm till his death in 1828. He was a Republican of the Jeffersonian stamp and a liberal in religious belief. He left two sons and daughters. His eldest son, Hon. Albert Steele, married Alice, daughter of Levi Love. His life was spent in Bridgewater. He died at the Center, where his venerable widow still lives. Robert Love owned the farm west of the Steele's, now owned by Mrs. John Clark. North of the Steele and Love farms, Capt. Zimri Howland leased 250 acres of John I. Morgan and John Delancey. Part of this lease he sold to Gresham Blackman and part, extending to the Unadilla, to Nathan Waldo. This is now owned by C. Beals, Mrs. Sarah Robinson and O. J. Clark. Zenas Gurley bought the farm east of the Steele's, now owned by C. Conklin. He came in 1776 and with him came Frederick Peirce, father of Hon. N. N. Peirce. Mr. Gurley died of the epidemic in 1810, leaving a widow and three children. One son, Henry, died in 1838; Harvey became a Mormon; Lavinia Morris, the daughter, lives in Chicago. Her daughter, Mrs. Thomas Avery, a most estimable and refined Christian lady, on her recovery from typhoid fever, became a victim of melancholia, and leaving her home came to Niagara and cast herself into the river at the verge of the falls. She left a letter to her husband, saying that the desire to save him and her family from the care of her alone prompted her action.

As with closed eyes and folded arms I sit in my easy chair

and "turn from all that is to what has been" and with mental vision pierce the veil of time the memory of the almost forgotten past, with its painfully pleasing and pleasingly painful pictures comes back to me and in fancy I see many of the busy actors of seventy years ago. The hardy pioneers in their homespun suits of linsey-wolsey or tow cloth as they slashed and burned the primeval forests. I see, too, the blackened stumps dotting the fields of corn, wheat, or oats. First, as is fitting, I recall Major Joseph Farwell, who opened the first farm on Farwell's Hill in 1789. With him came Ephraim and Nathan Waldo. The first house was framed of four crotches, roofed with split basswood, shingled with hemlock boughs, and clapboarded with blankets. In this improvised castle, just large enough to swing the proverbial cat, three families resided till midsummer. Then Farwell and Nathan Waldo moved into log houses. In 1790 Farwell built a sawmill on land now owned by W. J. Scott. In 1792 E. Waldo built a store and blacksmith shop on the hill. Mr. Thomas in the same year built a grist mill. Jerry Scott was the first miller. He married Nancy Wilson, aged 14 years. Her father lived on the knoll back of the house where James Taft now resides. She was the mother of ten children. Their average avoirdupois was a little less than our esteemed fellow citizen, W. S. Scott, who is one of them. E. Waldo built a house near where the South church now stands. In 1800 he sold to John Moon and moved to the Center. He was last seen at the battle of Queenstown Heights, October, 1872, at the foot of the cliffs. Whether he was killed or drowned in crossing to Lewistown is not known. Mr. Moon resided at the Waldo farm till his death in 1828 at the ripe age of 91 years. In 1834 the house was removed to make room for the church. John Moon had five sons, John, Henry, Peter, Jacob, and Philip. Jack and Phil were twins and had a fondness for corn juice and New England rum and from November till October the good people of Bridgewater were favored with at least three "full moons" each month, and not infrequently two in a single evening. Henry, Peter, and Philip died in Bridgewater at a good old age.

Deacon Asahel Hunt came to Bridgewater early in the 90's. In the winter of '94 he went to Coventry, Conn., returning in the spring with a helpmate. He owned the farm where T. Brown now resides.

March 5th, 1795, the town of Sangersfield was formed from Paris. It was named for Jedediah Sanger, who donated a barrel of rum for the honor. March 24th, 1797, Bridgewater was formed for the one chosen by the inhabitants by the member having charge of the bill, a native of Bridgewater, Mass. It is a misnomer, as there was, is not, and probably never will be, a decent bridge in the town.

On the 4th of April, 1797, when the town had arrived at the mature age of eleven days, the first town meeting was held at the tavern of Col. Thomas Converse. Thomas Brown, Esq., who, for two years, had been town clerk of Sangerfield, was clerk of the meeting. James Kuine presided in all the dignity of cocked hat, knee breeches, silver buckles, and dubbed queue. Clerk Thomas Brown certified the election of Thomas Brown as supervisor.

I was now 21 years of age, could read, write, and cipher, had my freedom, suit and Bible, but could not vote. A taxpayer might vote, a freeholder might hold office; I was neither. Of the freeholders who voted at this election the following have been supervisors: Thomas Brown, '97; James Kuine, '98, '99, 1800; Job Taylor, 1801 and '02; Asher Flint, 1803; Daniel Ringe, 1807, '08, '09, '10, '11, '12, '13; Peabody Fitch, supervisor in 1804, '05, '06, came to Bridgewater in 1800, purchasing the farm now owned by Deacon Howland. Taxpayers have ever been chronic grumblers since the day when the decree went out from Cæsar Augustus that all the world should be taxed, unless the impost is sugar coated and labeled "protection." Then mother's castor oil formula applies, "close your eyes, open your mouth, taken it down and call it good."

In 1796 there were 97 taxpayers in Bridgewater, real valuation, $1313.75; personal valuation, $3575.75 (total, $4889.50) tax, $118.18, average to taxpayer, $1.22. Ezra Parker, the landlord of the log hotel, on a valuation of $215 paid $5.18: Joe Loomis and Amasa Herrick each paid 19 cents, being the amount of tax on two cows of first and second quality.

During the eight years of pupilage the annual increase of population exceeded 125. They came from Massachusetts,

Rhode Island, and most of all from Connecticut, the land of steady habits, wooden nutmegs, and New England rum. They were young, few having seen thirty years. Many came with strong hearts, well trained muscles, a pack on their back and in their pockets the wherewith to buy a woodman's outfit—an axe. I venture to say that no town in the Whitestown country (the western half of New York) was settled by a braver, more enterprising or a more virtuous people than Bridgewater. Henceforth the increase in population was to be more slow, the lands were mostly in the hands of citizens, either by deed or permanent leases. Each week the openings were broadened; each year an increased amount of whiskey, wheat, and potash were sent to market. Carriages and buggies were not a prime necessity in those days. Most of the roads were mere winding paths among stumps, which were more numerous than milestones. Men on horseback with wives, sweethearts, or sacks of grain en croupe, were to be met at all hours. It was said of David Converse, Sr., who was noted for absence of mind, that, intending to take a grist to mill, he strode his horse and rode to mill with, as he supposed, the grist behind, as in truth it was—at his home. On one occasion, being thirsty, he tied his horse to a well sweep opposite the house of Abe Monroe and proceeded to lower the old oaken bucket into the well—he couldn't raise the horse.

Among the earliest settlers were Jesse, Joel, and Abner Ives. Jesse bought the farm on which his daughter now resides. In 1810 he moved to Whitestown, returning to Bridgewater in 1832. He voted for Abe Lincoln in 1860, dying a few days later.

Peter Pickett Truman and Solomon Blackman had farms north of the Steele brothers. In 1793 Abram Oaks bought a large track of land on Hardscrabble, building the house now owned by the Burton boys. Two hundred acres of the eastern portion he sold to Levi Carpenter and Eldred Peck. Supervisor Williams now owns a part of this. Capt. Hubbard settled the Pat Ryan farm. Elnathan Andrews bought of William Coxe the John Hook farm. Joe Loomis, Jr. owned the J. E. Jones place.

In 1798 the First Congregational church was organized by

Rev. Eliphalet Steele, of Paris. Meetings had been held in school houses and dwelling houses from the first settlement of the town. Daniel Converse and others read sermons. At the organization thirteen signed the covenant, seven males and six females. In less than five years there were sixty communicants. As natives of New England they felt there was a void that the meeting house alone could fill. In 1802 active measures were taken to fill the void. People of Paris, Plainfield, and Brookfield, co-operated. Sectarian feeling did not seal the pockets. In 1803 a church had been so far completed that it was opened for divine worship. The pastor at this time was Rev. James Southworth. A native of Montgomery Co., born in 1770, he commenced preaching in Warrensburg, that county, at the age of 21 years. In 1793 he removed to Burlington, Otsego county, preaching for four years in the Baptist church. In 1797 he preached to his first congregation in Rome. He came to Bridgewater in 1802, preaching there for 16 years and there he died in 1826. His successors in the pastorate were Rev's. Alpheus Miller, Hiram Kellog, who, for many years was identified with the schools in Clinton; Johnson Baldwin, and R. M. Davis. During Mr. Miller's pastorate Rev. S. W. Brace conducted revival services. He was an eloquent and graceful speaker and a haughty, overbearing man. After the retirement of Mr. Davis the society divided and in 1834 a new church was built in Bridgewater village. The next year a church was erected in Cassville. The division caused a bitter feeling in those who lived near the old meeting house. Dr. L. Hull sold out and left. The Benhams followed. The Halls would not contribute toward erecting the new house. Fred Pierce ceased to attend the church. When labored with, he declared he had not left the church, but the church him. The church was obstinate and he was cut off. In 1837, at the venerable age of 34 years, the old meeting house was demolished. In the winter of 1833–34, Stephen R. Smith, then of Clinton, and father of the Liberal Institute (later of Albany), preached in the new school house, where Mrs. Moses now resides. He was a clear, cogent, and eloquent speaker, and in one sermon the feeling of protest against the dogmas of Calvinism was crystallized.

A church, founded on the tenets of Hosea Ballou, was born,

and in 1834 the South Church was erected. L. C. Brown, Dolphus Skinner, Edward Wooley, and T. J. Smith, and others have filled its pulpit.

In 1805 the Congregational church bought of John Hopkins a grist mill and two acres of ground, west of Cassville, for $850. The toll was applied to the support of the pastor. Hence, I suppose that church stock, like railroad stocks, may be watered.

On the 12th of February, 1806, pursuant to notice, a meeting was held at the house of David Converse, Jr., where W. H. Briggs now resides, to organize a farmers' library, Rev. James Southworth presiding. By unanimous vote John Rhodes, James Southworth, P. Fitch, John Mott, and Laurens Hull were chosen trustees. Carefully selected books were procured.

These were not the days of steam and electricity, the mail did not fly over roads of iron, the electric fluid had not been taught to speed the thoughts of men on lines of steel, Robert Hoe had not invented the cylinder press, weekly papers from New York and the U. Patriot supplied them with news of the day. But English classics from that library—Pope, Addison, Steele, Young, Blair, Jonson, Bacon, Goldsmith, Gibbons, Plutarch's Lives, Discoveries in the Pacific by Magellen, Cook, Byron, Boygamville, and Portlock—read at the fireside, gave a higher tone of thought to the earlier citizens of Bridgewater than is possessed by the average community today. They had been taught in the common schools of Connecticut and prized them. While the state neglected its duty they, from their limited means, founded and supported schools in which the elements of an education could be obtained. Domini Avery, who taught a school near A. Monroe's more than 90 years ago, at the age of 80 had a head as white as mine at nearly 97. William Rider taught the same school in 1500–1510 and had a total attendance of 3,700 days. Mr. Everett, at the Center, in 1810 had an attendance of 5,830 days. He received from a rate bill, $42. State appropriations were small, so also was the school house. Like the old lady under the broom, the children needed elbow room. This was attained by a portion standing at their studies. In 1812 the towns of the state were districted. Gideon Hawley, in January, 1813, was first state superintendent. He held the office eight years.

Bridgewater Academy was incorporated by the legislature in 1826 and by the Regents in 1828. It was built by Tardius Denslow, and assessed in 1827, $1,000, tax, $2.64. Mr. James Deal, afterward a missionary of the American Board of Foreign Missionaries and Freelove, daughter of James Southworth, were early teachers. The academy stood on the premises now owned by H. P. Whitford, M.| D. For a time it flourished, but in a few years it lost its character and in 1838 ceased to exist.

In 1826 the Baptist church was organized with sixteen members. Its first pastor was Rev. A. Smith and in nine years its membership was increased to sixty. Jonathan P. Simmons succeeded him. During his pastorate the celebrated revivalist, Jacob Knapp, recruited the church by contract. In 1836 it had 114 members. In 1840 the church was moved from the hill to the east part of the village. Its candle shone brightly, but bright flames consume the substance. It has burned low, it flickers in the socket. Will it be permitted to expire?

In the early twenties the Friends built a meeting house at North Bridgewater. The doctrines of heresies of Elias Hicks split the meeting and the society ceased to exist. John Mott and Obadiah Williams, two of the members, were great-great-grandsires of Master Harry Marsh.

John Benham bought of John Collins and A. Monroe the Benham flats, 300 acres or more. This he deeded his son, James, for one peppercorn, and, becoming without support, became entitled to a United States' pension! John Rhodes rode on horseback to New York and obtained a deed of some hundred acres south of the Benham place and displaced a squatter who had no title. James Kinney bought of J. Benham. Asa, Oliver, and Martin Babcock were early settlers. Asa owned the farm in Paris from which George Chapman recently departed; Martin, the farm on which his son, C. H., now resides, Oliver, the Col. Peirce farm. Anthony Rhodes owned the Squire Rhodes farm; Ebenezer Parker owned the D. Worden farm, Peter Crandall, father of P. B. Crandall, owned the Gaughan farm, Peleg Brown owned the Alva Penny farm, Eldad Corbett owned the J. Terry farm. Den and Zerah Brown owned the Livermore place. Jedot Morgan bought of Amos Herrick the Dennis Shields' farm. South of this John and Isaac Mitchell, John Crowell, Samuel and Elias Jones owned. Ezra Parker came to town but a few days, if any, after Major Farwell.

James Kinney, E. Waldo, and Thomas Converse were the first justices appointed in 1798. Thomas Converse, the first grand juror, was fined $5 for non-attendance. Aaron Morse was member of assembly in 1803. Others were Levi Carpenter, Jr., L. Hull, J. Ruger, Samuel Woodworth, J. T. Trowbridge, N. N. Pierce, Peleg B. Babcock, A. Penny, Dewitt C. Little, John (for five years speaker) was born in the house where the tin shop now stands. Chief Justice Ruger first saw light in the house now owned by James O. Brown. Justice of the Supreme Court Rhodes, of California, was son of J. A. Rhodes, Esq. Leander Babcock, Member of Congress, from Oswego, was a native of Bridgewater. Mr. Taylor, an early settler, was Member of Congress from the southern tier. State Engineer and Surveyor John T. Clark, was a native of Plainfield; married and resided in Bridgewater.

Of seventy-nine persons who joined the Congregational church in 1819, Mrs. Alice L. Steele alone survives.

Our school fund was derived one half from the early liquor licenses and the other half from our share of the twenty towns laid out on the Chenango and Unadilla Rivers.

In 1832 Rev. Hiram H. Kellog removed to Clinton and built the Female Domestic Seminary. Board and tuition were $120 per annum. Work was furnished so that the cost might be diminished one-fourth to one-half. Mr. Kellog's methods were followed in Mt. Holyoke and Elmira Female Seminaries and the female department of Oberlin and Knox colleges. Mr. Kellog was first president of Knox College, Ill.

The story of the family, whose fowls had become so accustomed to moving, that when they saw the team attached to the covered wagon they lay on their backs and elevated their legs to be tied, slightly exaggerates the propensity to change that dominates the American people. The settlers of Bridgewater had their full allowance of quicksilver in their veins. Of the seventy different surnames on the tax list of 1786 but eleven are represented by descendents as residents today. Abram Oaks has two daughters living; Alice Steele represents the Love family; her two daughters represents the Love and Steele families; A. C. Waldo and sister, the Waldo family. Charlotte Ives, W. J. Scott, and Mrs. Ward the Ives family. Dewitt C. is grandson of Turman Blackman. A boy in his teens represents the Rhodes family. David Palmer is grandson of "Old" Jonathan Palmer. From collateral branches of the Palmer family tree are George William Palmer. Dea. Asahel Hunt was a grandparent of W. N. and M. T. Southworth and Mrs. James Tompkins. Mrs. Peabody Fitch is a granddaughter of L. Carpenter, Jr.; N. N. Peirce is a son of Fred Peirce, a citizen but not a taxpayer in '96. The grandfather of the venerable Oran Williams settled on a farm on the turnpike near Winfield. His neighbors were Bently and Samuel Guild. Simeon Pool took a contract in 1793 to carry the mail between Canajoharie and Whitestown, but sold to Jason Parker the same year and came to Bridgewater. Daniel Eels, one of the early farmers, carried a spade and musket at Bunker Hill. Asa Palmer, grandsire of our enterprising fellow citizen, W. W. Palmer, owned a farm on the hillside west of North Bridgewater. Job Tyler and Aaron Morse sold to John Mott in 1800 the farm now owned by Westland Parkinson. Asher Bull lived a little north of the house of G. Shaul, owning portions of the Shaul and Sholes farm. A Mr. Moore, grandsire of Dr. Moore, of Winfield, had a farm adjoining the Ives farm. Isaac Hall built a grist mill at Gooseville Corners. Eldad Peck built one on the Herson Hill farm. Nathan Waldo built a saw mill now owned by Henry Robinson. John Reckerson built a saw mill on the Evan W. Roberts farm, Elnathan Andrews, Jr., a saw mill at Gaskells Corners.

Sevres or Dresden porcelain did not grace the tables of the pioneers. Wooden trenches turned from ash blocks by Mr. Holcomb, at Gaskells Corners, or by Elizah Rice, on the Robert Williams farm, with burnished pewter platters and plates were appropriate to the rustic tables. Ebenezer Judson first opened up the farm of W. H. Brown, Esq. Ebenezer Moody gave the plat of ground and was the first tenant of the cemetery at the Center. Dr. Daniel Avery, who came to Babcock Hill with Anthony Rhodes, in 1792, was the first resident physician. He removed from the hill to the flat about 30 rods northeast of the

Center church, then to the farm now owned by J. D. Pierce and in 1814 to Leroy, Genesee county.   Of the 500 acres purchased by Maj. S. Rhodes a portion is now possessed by L. S. Brown. Major Rhodes sold it to a Mr. Langworthy, who deeded it to Loren Robbins, uncle of F. G. Robbins.   From his son, Clark, it came to Peleg Brown, or his son, L. Brown.

The highway leading from Shauls to North Bridgewater crossed the trout brook east of its present location.   At that crossing resided Benjamin Reynolds, grandsire of Mrs. George Ray.   Elias Bixby, who, on the night of July 15, 1779, carried a bayonet into Stony Point under ''Mad Anthony Wayne,'' lived and died where Mrs. Peter Chapin now lives.   His ashes lie in a nameless grave at the Center, while those of his grandson, whom he educated, and who died a millionaire, rest in Greenwood 'neath the shadow of a splendid monument on which many thousands were lavished.

Early in the '90's a framed tavern was erected at North Bridgewater by Mr. Lyman, where the cheese factory now stands.   In March, '98, $30 was paid for liquor license at $5 a license.   High license was not then a party cry.   Evolution had not then produced the prohibitionists.   While the town was in embryo, Abner Ives built a store where the U. V. R. R. office now is, at which farm produce and peltry could be exchanged for groceries, linsey woolsy, whiskey and New England rum. He sold to Plat Herrick, who converted it into a tavern.   For ninety years, excepting only when fire pumped that corner, liquor was always on tap.   In the hands of its present genial proprietor it has become a monument—a monument to departed spirits.

One hundred years is a brief period in a nation's life! One hundred years ago today the National Assembly of France was in convention.   The French revolution had commenced. One week from Saturday will be the centenary of the fall of the Bastile.   July 14, 1790, fourteen months after the inauguration of George Washington, the French constitution was adopted. Ninety years ago a mob broke out in the palace of Versailles, murdered the Queen's guards, compelled the King and Queen to return to Paris with the heads of the murdered guards carried on poles beside the state carriage.   Ninety-eight years ago the King and Queen fled from Paris, but were arrested and brought back. Ninety-seven years ago they were beheaded. Robespierre, Marat, the Reign of Terror, Napoleon in Italy, in Egypt, First Council, Council for Life, Emperor Austerlitz, Wagram, Elba, The 100 Days, Waterloo, St. Helena, Charles X, Louis XVIII, Louis Philippe, The Republic of '48, Louis Napoleon, Sedan, The 3rd Republic. All these events have transpired since Maj. Farwell laid his axe at the foot of the tree on the hill named for him.

NORTH BRIDGEWATER

AND EARLY SETTLERS OF ABOUT 1800

G. H. PARKHURST

That portion of Bridgewater, formerly and familiarly known as Benham's Flats, consists of a body of land at one time owned by Truman Benham, commencing at the foot of Babcock Hill by a long row of yellow willow trees running north on the borders of a little rivulet and embracing all the land now owned by Lorenzo S. Brown, opposite his residence, all the land owned by George H. Burgess; the lands owned by Wallace Randall, lying opposite of said Burgess; the old Benham homestead place, recently purchased by Irving Allen; the place now owned by Edwin Carpenter; the Michael Nugent farm, and sixty acres lying on the south side of the farm now owned by William W. Palmer, and running in a continuous body from said willow trees at the beginning of the above description to the Sauquoit creek, opposite of the Richfield Springs Junction depot and containing four hundred acres of as nice land as there is in the county of Oneida. About 1835 Mr. Benham sold this body of land to his son, Asahel, reserving about forty acres, being the original farm of said George H. Burgess. Soon after Asahel B. sold out the remainder to Oliver R. Babcock and the whole original four hundred acres were sold off and appropriated to different parties. The old gentleman remained but a short time and removed with the remainder of his family to the town of Lenox, Madison county, and his son to Wisconsin. Mr. Benham's oldest son, Milton, was the inventor of the art of conveying water through water-lime aqueducts. His first experiment was conducting water from lands now owned by George W. Palmer across the lands then owned by Joseph Budlong, Esq., to the old Benham homestead now owned by said Irving Allen.

The house so familiarly known as the Italian house at the

railroad crossing, was built about fifty-seven or eight years ago by David Barnum and he had a wagon shop on the opposite side of the road and carried on wagon making, but soon after sold out to Joseph Budlong, Sr., and moved to Cassville, built the shop where Davis & Barnum now carry on the business. This Italian house has a history, being the place where, a few years ago, a tragedy occurred in which one Italian shot another with a revolver, on Sunday, shooting through a window from the front side of the house, killing his victim instantly, in the presence of several others. He escaped and cleared the country. Sheriff Weaver afterward said that he had been informed that he was known to be in the city of London, England, but he was never apprehended and saved his neck from the gallows.

The place now owned by George W. Palmer was formerly owned by Hiram Marsh, who built the house in the summer of 1832, and was at that time engaged in the mercantile business, the store being a few feet north of the house. The upper portion of the store was conducted as a select school, it being the only select school at that time anywhere near, except the Academy at the village of Bridgewater. Mr. Marsh did not remain here in trade only a year or two after building the dwelling house, and removed the store and contents to Cassville and remained but a few years before the failure of Marsh & Stanley, and a week or two later the failure of Hiram followed. This left Calvin A. Budlong & Co. monarchs of the business at "Toad Hollow," as the place at that time was familiarly known, they having commenced trade there in the fall or winter of 1832. When Marsh moved to Cassville he sold his place to Gurdon Turner, who resided there till 1840, when he sold to Joseph Budlong, Esq., who, at that time, lived in the large square house on the east side of the road on the corner. Turner moved to the village of Bridgewater and died there, Budlong retaining this place till he died. His son, Jerome, then came in possession and afterwards sold to Joseph S. Rhoades and he sold to the present occupant, George W. Palmer in 1883.

The farm now owned and occupied by John B. Tuckerman was formerly owned by Abraham Monroe, who came here in an early day, purchased the land in the state of nature, cleared it up and built the present dwelling house there and conducted a country tavern, together with the farm for many years up to about 1832 or 1833. At this time Ezra Parker, who also was a pioneer, had built this large square house on the corner where the road leading from Fort Plain over Babcock Hill intersects the old Plank Road a few rods south of the Monroe house. At this time, when the country was new and full of emigrants from the eastern states seeking new homes, this road from Fort Plain over Paris Hill and to Clinton, was one of the main thoroughfares where the tide of emigration drifted, and tavern keeping in those days was quite a lucrative business. Monroe cut a road through the timber on his land from his house approaching the road leading to Babcock Hill in order to receive the traveling custom, thereby inducing them to come direct to his house instead of keeping the main road to the corner of the north and south thereby shunning the Parker tavern on the south corner. This Parker house is now owned by Mrs. Alex. Brown.

About 1796 or 1797 a log school house was built on the corner of Monroe's land. The late Esquire James A. Rhodes and Esquire Barnette, now of Clayville, (who then lived at Cassville) were among the little fellows who attended this school. This old gentleman related but a few years ago some of the anecdotes relating to their attendance. On one occasion the teacher punished a scholar by making him get down on all fours and put his nose through a knot-hole in the floor. Schools were few and scattering in those days and children were obliged to go two or three miles to reach these log school buildings, where they learned the rules and rudiments then commonly inculcated by backwoods pedagogues. This Monroe farm remained in the Monroe family till about the year 1854 or 1855 and was then purchased by George Tuckerman, the father of John B., the present owner and occupant.

The farm adjoining this on the north was owned by Elias Beers sixty years ago. He was a tailor by trade and carried on his farm and conducted his trade at the same time. He had three sons, Edwin, John and Charles. John went west many years ago and after the father's death, Edwin became the owner of the premises, afterward conveying them to Ebenezer Rider and he to James Potter, the present owner, who resides at Clayville and is engaged in the mercantile business. Beers, after selling to Rider, spent the remainder of his days in Cassville.

SOCIETY OF FRIENDS

A society of Friends, commonly called Quakers, at one time flourished at North Bridgewater and had a considerable membership. They built a commodious meeting house on the site where the cemetery is located at North Bridgewater and held meetings there for years, but finally became scattered and divided and so few remained that they in time disbanded. The house remained unoccupied for many years, was sold, taken down, and the timber removed to Clayville and put into a dwelling house now standing, and being the first house north of the Presbyterian church there. Obadiah Williams was quite a prominent member of this society and an early settler on the farm, well known, of late years, as the Alexander Brown farm, and after he became quite advanced in years sold out to Parmenas Mott in 1838, and, with the remainder of his family, left town. Mott soon after sold to Alexander Brown and moved to Cassville, where he was engaged in the mercantile business for a few years, but soon after retired from business and died in the city of Utica, leaving one son and two daughters: Wallace, Maria and Jane.

OTHER SETTLERS

David Miller settled on the farm now owned by Charles Green and was followed by Nathaniel Roberts. Roberts not only owned what is now Green's farm, but the fifty acres lying directly south of it, now belonging to Mrs. Margaret Brown, which he sold many years ago to Elisha Baker, Sr., and twenty-four acres adjoining this on the east side, he sold to Cornelius Dutcher. Roberts had six sons, Daniel, Amos, Ashael, Philo, Luman and Lyman, the latter being twins. Amos carried on the tanning and currying business at North Bridgewater in 1816 and perhaps a few years later. The tannery was located just back of the house now occupied by F. H. Spicer. Caleb Green and Calvin Smith followed him, and afterwards George Howe. John Mott settled, in an early day, on the farm now

owned and occupied by T. W. Parkinson. He had four sons
and five daughters. The sons were Joseph, John, Samuel
(elected sheriff of Oneida county in 1831) and Parmenas.
Joseph Converse married the daughter Sarah, who had two
children, Milton and Sarah Converse. One daughter married
Henry Thomas of Columbia, Herkimer county, and the other
three remained single.

THE OLD TAVERN

The old hotel premises has quite a history and perhaps it
might be somewhat interesting to some if the names of those
are mentioned from the first engaged down to the last who
kept, what in former days, was called a tavern. Tradition
claims this old tavern house to be the first or second framed
house erected in Bridgewater. A man by the name of Stone
was the first who opened the house to entertain the public
traveler, which must be sixty-five or seventy years ago, and
was followed by the following: Michael Foster, John J.
Mabbett, Brooks, Jotham King, H. C. Robins, G. T. Parkhurst,
Nelson Devendorf, Alonzo Brown, John Golden, Burch, Clark
Green and C. C. Green. A company was then formed by the
farmers in North Bridgewater and vicinity called the North
Bridgewater cheese and creamery company, who bought this
hotel property and conducted it as a stock company creamery
and cheese factory for several years, but it was afterward sold
to George A. Smith of Cassville, who has conducted it as a
cheese factory since, but has recently sold it to John Davis of
Cassville, who will continue the business by the aid of Lon
Brown, who has so successfully conducted the factory for the
past six years. Lon knows how to make good cheese and with
his genial good nature knows how to please the patrons with
his smiling countenance and a hearty good laugh, which cost
nothing but a pleasant disposition, letting nature develop itself.

VARIOUS INDUSTRIES

Artemus Newton, about seventy years ago, had a shop on
the corner near where James Malony's house now is; his main
business was wooding plows. Soon after Reynold Kirkland

carried on the same shop, employing a number of hands at the coopering business. He had several boys who learned the trade and worked with him. This was in the time when asheries and distilleries were quite extensively operated all over this part of the country and there was a great demand for potash and whiskey barrels, which made it quite a lucrative business in those days. The old gentleman moved his shop to Cassville with ox teams about 1835 and, as age and infirmities, together with hard work, necessitated him to soon after quit the business, he moved the remainder of his family to Jefferson county, where he finished his long journey of industrious life.

Jeremiah Brown, Jr., lived where Martin Malony does; had a cabinet shop, carried on the business and at the same time manufactured boots and shoes. Many years ago a man by the name of Wing owned the farm now owned by Mrs. Laura Randall, kept some very fine blooded stock horses; had a distillery across the road from Martin Malony's. John Mott once owned this farm, which, for many years after, was owned and occupied by Nicholas Rhodes, who had four sons and six daughters, of whom none are now living except Rosanna, who married Daniel Green. There was, at one time, no less than five or six asheries in this immediate neighborhood. In those days Cornelius Dutcher lived where Miss Hester Parkhurst does, having purchased the premises of one Parmalee, and owned about sixty acres of land now owned by Humphrey Roberts; had a blacksmith shop on the northwest corner of A. H. Parkhurst's lot, and, besides managing his farm, did quite an extensive business in the blacksmith shop. Esq. Peirce sold the lot where the blacksmith shop was the house lot to one Parmalee, and he to Dutcher. Joshua Babcock, Esq., who afterward lived for many years and died at Unadilla Forks, once owned the lot now owned by A. H. Parkhurst, together with ten acres lying on the south side of J. R. Moses' place, and carried on the saddle and harness business for several years. The late Henry Babcock and his sister Lucy were born here. Babcock sold to Peirce and Peirce afterwards purchased the north part of the land now owned by said Moses. A man by the name of Hammond once lived in a log house between where Moses' house now stands and the barn. A man by the name of Walton followed Hammond. Peirce sold to Newcomb, who carried on the cabinet business and other shop work and died here. After his death the place was purchased by Jeremiah Brown, Jr., and Brown afterwards sold to Esq. Peirce, making twice Peirce became the owner. After this Peirce lived in the Moses house till his death, which occurred about forty-three years ago. He owned a farm on the west hill containing about eighty acres and that he purchased of the Rev. James Southworth, being a part of the farm now owned by John F. Jones. Mr. Peirce was one of the early settlers of Bridgewater, was a carpenter by trade and quite extensively known as a surveyor, did all the business in that line in early days. He surveyed every highway in town; his record as such is filed in the town clerk's office of the same. Peirce had two sons and four daughters, none now living except Olive, who married a Brooks, and Col. N. N. Peirce, who has been respectfully mentioned in a foregoing chapter. Dutcher sold the house and lot now owned by Miss Hester Parkhurst to Jonas Monroe and he to George P. Oatly and it was afterward conveyed to G. H. Parkhurst.

James Height, sixty years ago, lived where John Downs does and was engaged in manufacturing hats and had a shop in the building now occupied as a dwelling house and owned by Milton Tripp, but moved many years ago to Bridgewater village and conducted the business there till modern improvement for such tradesmen compelled those of the old style of manufacture to quit the business in our towns and villages and the business went into large establishments.

Esq. Peirce sold the place now owned by A. H. Parkhurst to a man by the name of Hickox, who was engaged in the sale of clocks in the year 1832 and fled to the country from the city of Utica when the cholera scare entered there, and made this purchase and the next year built the present upright of the house connecting it to the old original house, making it a wing to the new part. Hickox did not remain here but a few years, going back somewhere in New England where he came from.

Our postoffice was established in 1850 and Elisha Baker

was its first postmaster and the present incumbent is Thomas
Parkinson.

NOTE—Present occupants and owners of places mentioned in above
sketch: Lorenzo Brown place, Charles Clark; George Burgess place, George
Burgess; Wallace Randall lands (opposite George Burgess'), Wallace Randall;
Irving Allen (old Benham homestead), George Burgess; Edwin Carpenter's
house, Mrs. Edwin Carpenter, (occupant, Del Knapp); Michael Nugent farm,
Del Bush; Wm. Palmer farm, H. A. Palmer, (occupant, John Owens); George
W. Palmer's lands and place, Mrs. George W. Palmer; location of old Italian
house, railroad crossing and Babcock Hill road; Davis & Barnum business in
Cassville, John Davis, (occupant, Sidney Davis); place of business of Marsh,
Budlong, Rhoades, Palmer, now a dwelling owned and occupied by Menzo
Tripp, (when a store it stood opposite I. M. Risley's house in Cassville; Ezra
Parker's tavern (large square house, owned by Mrs. Alex Brown), Mrs. Alex
Brown, (occupant, Charles Brown); James Potter farm, James Potter.

NOTE—Present owners and occupants of places mentioned in above
sketch: Alexander Brown farm, Mrs. Alexander Brown; Charles Green farm,
Mrs. Frank T. Jones; E. H. Spicer house, Bert I. Brown (used as tenant
house); T. W. Parkinson farm, old stock company creamery, old hotel now,
run as such by Clayton Town; James Malony's house, Mrs. John McIlheny;
(occupant, Perkins); Martin Malony's house, Mrs. Martin Maloney, (occupant,
James Town); Mrs. Laura Randall's farm, W. N. Randall; Miss Hester Parkhurst's place, bought and occupied by A. H. Parkhurst; John F. Jones' farm,
owned by F. J. Southworth; John Down's house, Mrs. Walter Lusby; house
owned and occupied by Milton Tripp, Andrew Knauer; last postmaster and
when postoffice was disbanded, Thomas Parkinson, 1902.

BABCOCK HILL

G. H. PARKHURST

Asa and Oliver Babcock from North Stonington, New London county, Conn., were among the first settlers on the hill and from them it received its name.   Asa came in 1797 and settled on the farm in the town of Paris on the town line of Bridgewater and Paris, it being the farm now owned by George Chapman.   This farm joins the one in Bridgewater upon which Oliver Babcock located in 1797, the latter now the property of Col. N. N. Peirce of Bridgewater village.   Martin Babcock, the younger brother of the two, came to the town in 1807, and located on the farm now owned by his son, Clark H. Babcock. He purchased of Roland Stiles who had made the first improvements on the place.   None of these three were married at the time of settlement.   Asa was a cabinet maker by trade and erected a shop upon his premises, in which he carried on the business for some time, but finally discontinued the business and gave his time and attention exclusively to farming.   Martin did some work in the cooper line.   Asa originally took up two hundred acres of land, Martin's place contained one hundred. Oliver commenced with a small amount, but in after years became a large land holder.   The first trips of these brothers to this region were made on horseback.   Martin and Oliver both served in the army during the war of 1812, the former being stationed at Ogdensburg and the latter at Sacketts Harbor. Both of them died before the act granting pensions to the soldiers of 1812 was passed.   Asa Babcock had three sons and a daughter: Lorin, Leander and Augustus, and the daughter married S. H. Reynolds.   Leander was a graduate of Union College at Schenectady, read law with Esquire Willard Crafts of Utica and afterwards became a very popular lawyer in the city of Oswego; served his people in the thirty-second Congress in 1851–1852.   Augustus was assassinated by Edward Varndell on the morning of December 27, 1835, at the old home place. The assassin, in a fit of maddened jealousy, beat out his brains with the head of an ax in early morning while he lay sweetly reposing in his bed. Varndell then returned to the room, which he and his wife occupied, and struck her while she was sitting in her chair before the blazing fire partially dressed, killing her, then cut his throat from ear to ear in the same room, killing himself almost instantly. This was one of the greatest tragedies that ever occurred in this part of the country. Augustus was but twenty-two years old when he met this untimely doom.

Oliver Babcock had two sons and two daughters, Oliver R. and Peleg B., Maria and Clarissa. Oliver R. represented the town of Bridgewater in the board of supervisors in 1843 and 1844 and twice in the town of New Hartford. Peleg B. was quite extensively engaged in farming. He served his town in the board of supervisors from 1851 to 1854. He was elected and served as Member of Assembly in 1857, was taken sick while in the Legislature, came home and did not live but a few days. Babcock Hill and Bridgewater lost one of its most worthy citizens and he has been missed by his host of friends. Maria married Albert Burke and Clarissa became the wife of S. H. Reynolds.

Martin Babcock had two sons and three daughters, Clark H., who now resides and owns the old home farm, and Henry, who lives in Florida. Elizabeth married Giles Scott of Brookfield, Catherine married Myron Scott, who died soon after marriage and his widow died in Florida a short time ago. Kaziah married J. Jerome Budlong, who now resides at Aurora, Ill.

Major Anthony Rhodes, a veteran of the Revolution and a resident of North Stonington, Conn., came to this town with his family in 1792. His wife was an aunt of the before mentioned Babcocks. He purchased a five hundred acre lot of land of Judge Sanger of New Hartford. This land was then all in its wild state of nature. Not a house, a public road, or an inhabitant in sight or hearing. The Major built a log shanty on the place (Babcock Hill) and then returned east after his family, which he moved by ox team the following year and settled them in this rude log building, being but a few rods from where the present dwelling house now stands which is the same built by him a few years after.

The roads were nothing but winding foot paths among forest trees and fallen timber. His son, James Avery Rhodes, Esq., was born in Connecticut in 1790 and was consequently but two years old when brought to this town. James A. Esq., always resided at this place where his father built the house, 1806, with the exception of a few years at Clayville, and died here in 1886, being ninety-six years old. He was several times elected and officiated as Justice of the Peace and held the office of Supervisor for the first time in 1824 and again in 1840. The father, Anthony, moved many years ago to a farm near North Winfield, Herkimer county, where he died at quite an advanced age. Maj. Rhodes' wife was a sister to Capt. Oliver Babcock, who came this way at some time during the Revolution with a small band of Connecticut soldiers. They proceeded from Schenectady to what is known as the "Carr farm," named Carr from an Indian agent in Otsego county, and thence up the Unadilla and down the Oriskany to Fort Stanwix. On the way they camped on the very ground which was afterwards selected by Major Rhodes as a home. Capt. Babcock mentioned this place to his brother-in-law after his return to Connecticut and the latter came down and bought it, settled here and he and his wife are now buried upon it.

John Rhodes, a brother of the Major, about the same time came here and purchased a large amount of land of a man by the name of Beach in the city of New York, and went then, riding on horse back, to procure his deeds. He had five sons, Dr. Rhodes, who practiced medicine on Babcock Hill in quite an early day, Nicholas, who settled at North Bridgewater, Rev. James Rhodes, who used to administer the gospel to the Baptists at Cassville, Esquire Benjamin and Capt. Sion. A part of this lot of land purchased by John Rhodes consisted of the land or farm that Benjamin Rhodes owned and occupied till his death, which occurred in 1853 and now owned by Franklin Leonard; the farm now owned by Square S. Shawl and for many years by Capt. Sion Rhodes; quite a large portion of Newton Sholes farm and about forty acres owned by Wallace Randall.

Asa Babcock built a hotel on Babcock Hill in 1812 and carried it on till he died about 1825. Simeon Green rented it afterwards for seven years and kept it till the spring of 1832. It was afterward kept as a hotel for many years, Lemuel J. Tripp being the last, who is the present owner, but has not kept it as a public house for several years.

The first store at this place was kept by Parmenas Mott, and afterwards by Rhodes & Robbins and they at the same time carried on an ashery near where the school house now stands. Others have been in the mercantile business here but no one at the present time.

There was a tavern house where E. L. Austin's house and shoe shop now stands. A man by the name of Budlong owned the place, who had three sons and several daughters, Esquire David, who resided at Cassville; Capt. James, who afterwards owned the farm now owned by William Walsh, and John Budlong. One of the daughters married Horace Luce, one Benjamin Bentley, one a man by the name of Osendorf and another David Barnum. Budlong sold the farm to Stukely Allen about 1838 or 1839 and Allen a few years after sold to Peleg B. Babcock. Simeon Green was an early settler on the farm now owned by Mr. Bailey. He carried on the farm and opened a stone quarry, burned lime, got out flagging and step stones and at one time made it quite a business. He had a large family, consisting of seven sons and four daughters: Samuel, Daniel, Jonathan, Benjamin, Clark, Charles and Alonzo; Margaret, Eunice, Lydia and Mary Ann. None are now living except Charles.

Babcock Hill has a postoffice which was established in 1845 with Dr. John H. Champion as its first postmaster. E. L. Austin is the present incumbent.

The physicians that have settled here and practiced medicine are Drs. Rhodes, the elder Maine, his son, Oliver, Erastus Kind, and last, John H. Champion.

A man by the name of Hatfield settled on the farm now owned by Lawrence Dugan. Elisha Wetmore, who was well known as a tavern keeper on Frankfort Hill, married one of his daughters and two of the Hatfield sons married sisters of Wetmore and settled in Iowa.

James A. Rhodes, Esq., had three sons and two daughters, James Anthony Rhodes, the eldest son, went to California several years ago and is now engaged in horticulture and growing fruit. Augustus is a lawyer by profession. He received his primary education at the district school on Babcock Hill and prepared for college at the academy at Bridgewater village and after graduating at Hamilton college at Clinton, went to Indiana, where he read law and after having been admitted to the courts there went to California. He was at one time one of the Supreme Court Judges and since his retirement from the Court has been engaged in his profession. William, the youngest son, died while in business in New York city ten or twelve years ago, leaving a widow and a bright young boy, who both now remain at the old homestead. Mary Ann, the oldest daughter, married Henry O. Southworth, who was a lawyer by profession and was of the popular firm of Pomeroy & Southworth in the city of Rome, Oneida county, for a number of years, but on account of failing health the firm dissolved. Afterwards Southworth practiced some in the city of New York, but failing again in health was obliged to retire from work and lived but a short time after. The death of the wife in a few years followed. Susanna married a lawyer by the name of Miner who lived in California near Judge Rhodes and is conducting his profession.

The farm at the foot of Babcock Hill and now occupied by Capt. Lorenzo S. Brown, whose mother was a sister to the Babcocks, is the place where Major Lorin Robbins settled in an early day. He was a veteran soldier of the Revolution, having enlisted as a fifer at the age of fourteen. He told many revolutionary tales and one in particular which he related made its lasting impression. He had been out upon one occasion with a company of privates and been successful in capturing a British merchant vessel which proved to be a very valuable prize. The crew surrendered without a gun being fired or a wound given. The vessel and crew were anchored in the harbor at New London, Conn. The Major stayed over night at a hotel in the place that he might be on hand the next day to receive his portion of the booty. But when early morning came a British fleet was discovered lying in sight of Fort Griswold, which was then garrisoned by militia hastily summoned from the labors of the field. The British landed their troops and hastily assaulted on three sides at the same moment. The garrison fighting in view of their property and their homes made a brave and obstinate resistance. By the steady and well-directed fire, many of the assailants were killed. But pressing forward with persevering ardor the enemy entered the fort through the embrasures. This put an end to all resistance. Irritated by gallantry which should have caused admiration a British officer inquired who commanded the fort. "I did," said Colonel Ledyard, "but you do now," and presented him with his sword. The Briton seized it and savagely plunged it into Ledyard's bosom. This appeared to be the signal for an indiscriminate massacre. Of one hundred and sixty men composing the garrison, all but forty were killed or wounded and the most of them after resistance had ceased.

Seldom has the glory of victory been tarnished by such detestable barbarity. The enemy then entered New London, which they set on fire and consumed it. The property they destroyed was immense. They likewise set fire to the vessel taken by the privateers mentioned and together with its cargo was burned to the water's edge. The Major, after the enemy left, went into the fort and was an eye witness to the most cruel acts performed during the whole siege of the Revolution and lost his anticipated realization of the great prize so nobly taken the day before. All this the old Major would relate with a saddened spirit, now and then raising his trembling hand to his glistening eyes to wipe away the tears that trickled down his aged and furrowed cheek, which sprang from the heart as he called to mind the melancholy scenes of his dead companions as they lay there in sight of their dear homes, and the ones they held most dear to their hearts, butchered while manfully defending their homes and country.

The old elm tree, standing in the center of the highway which divides the line between L. S. Brown and George H. Burgess has been a landmark for nearly a century. This huge old giant tree like Og, the king of Bashan, the remnant of giants of his race, is now visibly fast going to decay. Stephen Adams, an early settler, related that he had occasion to stop near this tree when it was not more than eighteen inches through and struck the bit of his ax in the side of it which left a scar now plain to be seen. It now measures eighteen feet around the trunk, three and one-half feet above the ground.

NOTE—Present occupants and owners of places mentioned in above sketch: George Chapman farm, Mrs. Byron Randall; Col. N. N. Peirce property, Fred Peirce (son of N. N. Peirce); Clark Babcock farm, owned by Fred Ludermann; house built by Major Babcock, Clark Babcock farm; Franklin Leonard farm, Mrs. James McDermont; owner of old hotel, Lemuel Tripp; store conducted at Babcock Hill, Lester B. Sheridan; E. L. Austin's house, Lester B. Sheridan; Wm. Walsh farm, Walsh brothers (William, John, Thomas); Peleg Brown farm, Lorenzo Brown farm; Bailey farm, Henry Bailey; last postmaster, Miss Ida Miller; present system, R. F. D.; Lawrence Dugan farm, Maggie Dugan (the house on the Lawrence Dugan farm was burned about 1900. Thomas Dugan, aged about 40 years, son of Lawrence Dugan, was burned to death in the fire The house has not been rebuilt); Cap. Lorenzo Brown farm, Charles Clark.

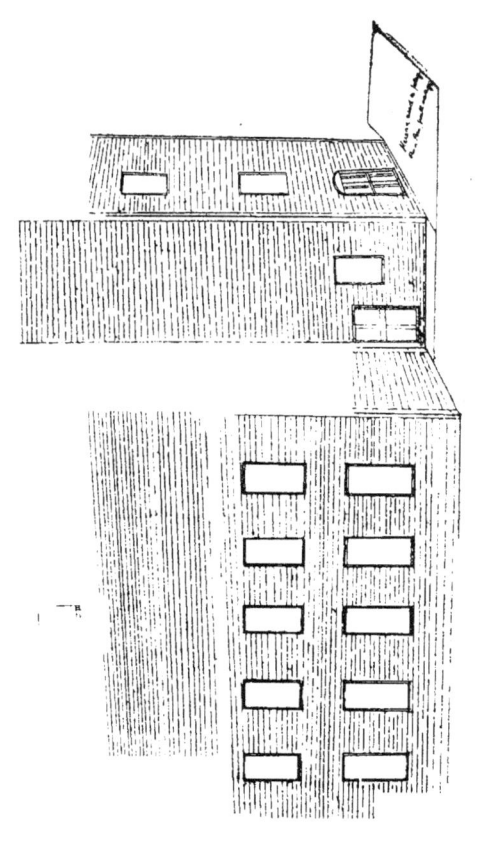

The accompanying illus-
tration was taken from a
pencil drawing by the late
William N. Southworth
and is preserved as the
only existing representa-
tion of the old Center
Church. This sketch was
made entirely from mem-
ory and is given just as left
in his original drawing.
A fine description of this
building is found in Mr.
Southworth's story of the
Center Church.

THE OLD CENTER CHURCH

The following is a most interesting and carefully prepared history of the old Congregational church which stood at Bridgewater Center near the Briggs' residence. This building was torn down in 1837, part of the timber forming the present church in the village. Inspired by the Centennial celebration of the Congregational church Mr. South-worth drew from a remarkable and wonderful memory a vision of the old structure as it existed and wrote a sketch in the form of a letter to a close friend and this letter was read at this celebration June 29, 1898. At the same time he prepared a rough draught of the building entirely from memory thus preserving, what would otherwise have been lost sight of, a picture of those old days. His style is charming and his quick wit and finely expressed thoughts have furnished for this generation a wonderful presentation of a historical setting of past days.

May I present to you a picture from the retina of memory of the Old Meeting-house at the Centre? Well! In imagination stand beside me at the north front door of Mr. Briggs' dwelling house. Before us is the "Green," a Common two acres in extent. In front of us, about seven rods away, is the Steeple 16 feet square and more than 80 feet high. To the left, commencing in line with Mr. Briggs' house, are the Meet-ing-house sheds extending to the Gooseville road.

On this June Sabbath of 1834, while the choir are singing Old Hundred or Hebron, we will walk around to the Meeting-house and glance at the exterior. Notice how close the sward is clipped, and yet we have no patent lawn mowers. We have cows, swine with jewels in their noses, and geese; these are free commoners. Of all domestic animals on the farm, none clip so close to the ground as the goose, except the ganders, and one-half of these geese are ganders.

In almost every stall of the sheds we notice a lumber wagon, double or single; we see saddle horses tied to the braces. No buggies, no steel springs; steel springs have not come to B— as yet. Many wagons have the wagon chair in front, three armed and splint bottomed. These are for the old folks. Younger people are content with cleated boards, placed cross-wise the box or go on foot. Some of us washed our feet Sunday morning and went to meeting barefoot. If the families were large and lived at a distance from the Meeting-house the smaller fry sat in lap or were sandwiched between the knees of the elders.

Large families were not uncommon in those days. J. W. Whitfield, who preaches now and then, writes for the papers now and then and wrote "Now and Then" for the Centennial, had for his first wife Harriet the 12th and youngest child of Cornelius Dutcher. "Deacon Dutcher" is now (1834) living in the red house opposite John J. Mabbett's hotel at North Bridgewater. Note. "Now and Then" a poem of 100 stanzas "like linked sweetness, molasses candy, long drawn out."

There are two vehicles in the shed that require a passing notice. These are the coach of Levi Bostwick and the carriage of Truman Benham. Mr. Bostwick built the hotel in B— (Saunders). When he sold out he retained his family coach; an oval box on thorough braces covered with leather. Had we been on the Meeting-house steps at 10:30 A. M. this morning we might have seen the coach leave the highway, and crossing what will be the dooryard of W. H. Briggs and drawing up at the steps there alighted Mr. and Mrs. Levi Bostwick and Becca and Nancy and Hattie and Maria and Willard and Warner; then the coachman, "Bostwick's nigger," drove the equipage to the B. shed. Next came the Truman Benham carriage with Mr. and Mrs. Benham and Miles and Milton and Azael and Clarissa and her sisters. Children, like others, judge from the outward appearing; so judging, we conclude the two B's. are the richest men in town. The B. of Bridgewater is richer than the B. of Benham Flats, for the first has a "nigger driver," the second has not.

The Meeting-house is east of us. Its dimensions are 60 feet by 40. It stands on a wall 3 feet high of unhammered stone. On this side are 10 windows, 32 panes, 8 x 10. On the north is a single window, a pointed or Gothic arch. The window sill is 14 feet from the ground. On the east side are 9 windows. At the center of the lower tier is a sand stone colored door, approached by 4 steps guarded by banister and newell. We will not enter here. The benediction has been given and the worshipers are making their exit from the front doors. Now the last wagon and the last gossip have gone. We come to the front. As the ground slopes a little the wall here is but 2 feet high. One step to the broad platform, two steps to the folding doors, which have not been closed, and we enter the vestibule; seven or eight steps and we pass through folding doors into the auditorium at the foot of the broad aisle. At the north end of the aisle is the pulpit, flanked on either side by flights of stairs supported in front by turned pillars; upholstered in green velvet with cords and tassels. On the center of the pile is the Meeting-house bible. With reverence and curiosity we walk up the aisle. We glance at the pews. They are 6 feet by 5, sides paneled and perpendicular, with a black semi-circular rail. There are seats on both sides and at the rear end. When the pew is filled, nearly one-half the sitters face the pulpit, nearly one-half face those who face the pulpit, the balance turn the shoulder to the pulpit. When near the pulpit, you turn to the right, I to the left, walk about 14 feet, turn at right angle, down the side aisles, another turn, and we meet near the entrance. Again in the vestibule we turn to the right or left and face doors of exit.

If you are tired of my picture or my company, say so and say good by. If you wish to see more, turn your face south, I will do the same, go up ten or eleven steps to a broad stair, turn inward and we meet face to face; up one step, then shoulder to shoulder we mount four steps. There is room on these stairs for six abreast. In our walk below we compassed thirty-two pews. We also passed twenty-four wall pews. At the center on either side two pews are wanting. Here are two huge box stoves. We notice the galleries. They are on three sides. They overhang the side aisles and are supported by square pillars placed in the angles of the body pews. But we have got up stairs. Folding doors admit us to the galleries. Turning right and left respectively we walk to the upper end. We are in line with the minister. On the wall side of the aisle, which is very narrow, we can open the door of one of the wall pews, up two steps and enter—the pews are like those below except that naughty boys have carved their initials and grotesque figures on the panels. Down a couple of steps on the other side of the aisle to the singers' seats. As they extend on three sides of the Meeting-house they will accommodate 60 people. There are 28 wall pews. We now notice over the entrance 2 high pews supported by pillars and reached by a flight of stairs. These were known by me as "nigger pews." Till 1828 there were slaves in B— and these pews were set for their accommodation. I long since set this down as an idle tale. On Centennial Day I spoke to Eunice Robinson about it. She said the story was a true one, she having herself seen the colored people sitting there. I was also told that some officer of the meeting sat there to overlook the young folks and report if they behaved improperly.

As we are sitting in the gallery we notice the ceiling. It is on a plane with the plates. It is supported by turned pillars on the breast works, thence it curves upward 5 feet, supported by wide studding sawed from "natural crooks." The balance is horizontal.

On the front of the high pews we note the figures 1805. These tell the year in which Gurdeon Turner finished the joiner work. As we again enter the steeple, we notice in the angle at our left a narrow door. We open it; a long, steep stairway leads to the loft above. I have been told that this story is 18 feet high. It looks about that does it not? Loose boards are only an apology for a floor, so be careful where you step. Up another and shorter stairway—flooring like that below. I place a ladder on one of the boards. The upper end of the ladder in the scuttle hole. Climb the ladder and remove the scuttle. You are just beneath the bell. Sway the clapper gently; the tone is very good. Strike it forcibly; you are half deafened. Come onto the bell deck. For many years the steeple extended no higher. Timothy Badger was the bell ringer. I knew him well. Inflamed eyes and face, great in girth, a perfect Jack Falstaff. The bell was rung at 9 A. M. and 12 M. on week days, and on Sunday told the hours for Divine Service. Waterbury, Elgin and Waltham watches are not known as yet. We laboring people find our appetites when Tim rings the noon bell which seldom varies more than fifteen minutes. While Tim was on duty one day there was a crash and the bell and its tones were both cracked. The bell was recast and the steeple was completed. So my description is not.

We now stand in a hexangular structure about 15 feet high,

boarded on its six sides with an opening 20 inches wide and 5 feet high on each side to give free course to the tone of the bell. Now step on that block; place your shoe with your foot in it on the window sill. Let me have your glove with your hand in it. Spring lightly down; no fear of falling, that rail is 2½ feet high and is pretty firm. Look down 55 feet. That man staring up at us appears to have stopped growing in his "early teens." Walk around the tower. Admire the landscape. Hills and plains, forests and fields, meadows and pastures, fields of corn, wheat, rye and oats. Not a hop yard. We do not drink beer, except domestic root beer. Cider from our apples, whiskey from our rye and Old Jamaica or New England rum are good enough for us.

As we change our point of view, the varied and variegated landscape appears a huge crazy quilt or lovely panorama and you exclaim "Oh, it's just perfectly lovely!" and I remark 'tis rather pretty. Now place your back to the railing, crane your neck backward, at a height of 15 feet is another railing; it is about 20 feet high. Within this, surrounded by a narrow ledge, the hexagon sloping inward rises about 12 feet. You can get to this ledge by climbing the lightning rod. Don't do it if you are subject to dizziness.

Above this sloping tower is the "tin," a pyramid 5 feet high with 3 1-3 feet base and from the apex a spire 6 feet high arises. A vane 5 feet long in the form of an arrow, gilt at one end, painted at the other, indicates the direction of the wind. This is set off by gilt balls, one above, one below. Before the Meeting-house became disused the upper ball slid down onto the vane and set it.

Two years hence (in 1836) with a parcel of school children we may stand at the foot of the steeple and see a boy of eighteen climb the rod and raise that ball and wedge it to its place and descend unhurt. The lightning rod, made by the village blacksmith, consisted of pieces of iron about 6 feet long with an eye at one end and a hook at the other was hooked into the spire, bent to conform to the tower, and passing from the eaves of the belfry and down to the steps, through a hole in the plate-form into the top of a pine or cedar post. It lacked a foot of reaching the ground. I cannot say that electricity, greased or ungreased, ever took that route. But my mother once told me that one of the Ward girls said she saw a ball of fire as large as a peck measure go down the rod. When a little tot I had seen on the Fourth of July, fire balls. It seemed a wonder to me how so large a ball could pass through an augur hole. Saturday evening, which in accordance with Pilgrim usage we kept, father had told me of Jonah and the fish, Sampson and the jaw bone, Joshua and the ram's horn, and Jericho and Daniel and the lions, S. M. & A. and the fiery furnace, so I accepted the ball of fire. *I never doubted my mother's word.*

Go down the way you came. I'll go down the lightning rod and meet you on terra firma. Farewell, Ghost of the Meeting-house on the Green! You and the generation that once worshiped in you are but a mere memory. Sixty-one years ago Elery Woodworth pulled down the edifice and the Green is *Noctes Campos Vaccinos.*

Please allow me to present to you Rev. Edward Allen. Like Moses of old he is an austere man. Calvinism is ingrained in his nature. I think I never saw him smile. He came Sept. 1835 with a wife and two sons, John aged 11 years and George 9. They lived in the H. E. Palmer house.

In the spring of 1836 the great Baptist revivalist, Elder Jacob Knapp, held a Union protracted meeting in the North Church. His sermons were of the composite order, nine parts of the lightnings and thunders of Sinai and one part of the Gospel of Love. Evening after evening the church was crowded. Some people were excited to the verge of insanity. The "Anxious seats" were crowded with tearful, sobbing, groaning penitents. The Baptists got most of the converts. Many when the excitement was passed fell from grace. Of the converts I fondly recall the names of John Allen and his friend and my friend John Monroe. Other young people, my school mates, were Frank Curry, who lived with Mott Otterhouse, Erastus Perkins in the S. Clark house; John M. lived in the Bebb house, and Caroline Scott of Scott Street. A finer set of young people I never knew.

In May, 1837, E. Perkins was drowned in the Mohawk, aged 13. August after, Caroline Scott died, aged 14. John Allen while preparing for college died aged 16. Frank Curry died in his teens in Illinois. He was receiving a salary of $500 per year. John Monroe, learning the printer's craft, died in Rome. On a slab in the Center graveyard you can read "John Monroe. Died Nov. 7, 1845. Aged 21 years. He desired to serve God in the ministry on earth, but was called to serve Him in heaven. Erected by his young friends as a memorial of love."

* * * * * * * * *

Having finished my task I'll change my subject and "Tell a story" or two of the Rev. Jeddediah Burchard* One of these I have heard told by the late Albert Steele. Mr. Steele was teaching school in Jefferson County. He attended a meeting at which the eccentric Rev. J. B. preached and heard him tell this story of a brother cleric who at family prayers always stood with hands resting on a chair back and in the earnestness of his petition would move himself and chair about the room. There was a trap door that opened to the cellar. One morning the trap door had been incautiously left open, or perhaps cautiously opened by his sons. The good man in his earnestness shoved the chair into the hole. Chair and man landed in the cellar. One of the graceless sons, clapping his hands in glee, exclaimed "There! The devil has given Dad a fall!" A young man of the congregation as the story ended seeing it from a ludicrous point, exploded with laughter. The Rev. J. B., shocked at the ill-timed levity, exclaimed, "Young man, don't laugh at those ungodly boys!" Mr. Steele said he restrained his risibles by stuffing his bandana in his mouth.

It is related that Mr. Burchard had for winter wear a pair of buckskin breeches. These in warm weather were stored. On a cold day in early winter he went to the garret and encased so much of his person in this garment as it was intended to cover and repaired to the Meeting-house. Suddenly while making the first invocation he stopped and violently slapping his breeches on the flanks, front and rear, exclaimed, "Bretherin, the word of the Lord is in my mouth, but the devil is in my breeches!" A colony of wasps had taken possession of the garment in the summer and the irascible insects resented his intrusion into the premises which they had held by peaceful possession.

* Mr. Burchard was a preacher at Camden, N. Y.

UNIVERSALIST CHURCH

CONGREGATIONAL CHURCH

HISTORY OF CHURCHES

CONGREGATIONAL CHURCH

This society was organized March 8, 1798, with thirteen members. In 1805 a house of worship was erected two miles north of the village, located between Harrison Briggs' house and the corner. In this building meetings were held until 1835 when the church was divided and a new society formed at the village, at which time the present edifice was erected.

Then, as now, from the hall you entered the church by doors on either side, but between them, where the double doors are now, was the pulpit. Doors closed at the end of each box-shaped pew and were securely buttoned on the inside. A gallery went around the entire church, having box seats like the audience room and over the pulpit was one gallery larger than the others. The choir occupied the farther end of the gallery opposite the pulpit and when their part of the service came they were started off by the aid of a tuning fork. Later a reed organ became one of the church's proud possessions.

About 1876 there were great changes and the interior was altered to the present style and arrangement and a new pipe organ was placed in the church. In the year 1889 cathedral glass windows replaced the small glass ones. This was the prevailing condition until 1902 when further improvements were made by the addition of a dining room and kitchen in the rear. The old time box stoves were removed and a furnace put in. The entire interior was newly decorated and newly furnished. To these improvements were added communion table and chairs and the church presented a very attractive appearance. June 29, 1898, a centennial celebration was held and most interesting meetings followed. Following is the list of pastors in the order which they served: James Southworth, Alpha Miller, H. H. Kellogg, R. M. Davis, Edward Allen, Seth P. M. Hastings, Charles Machin, Edward Allen (second time), S. W. Brace, H. Boynton, Dr. Gamage, J. W. Whitfield, Moses Thatcher, William B. Thompkins, C. H. Beebe, F. Bradnack, L. W. Church, J. S. Upton, John Marsland, Charles W. Drake, Samuel Manning, Nathan S. Aller, Aurelian Post, Charles Fraser, Nathan S. Aller (second time), Edw. C. Wiley.

UNIVERSALIST CHURCH

On March 4th, 1833, several inhabitants of Bridgewater, Brookfield and Plainfield met at the house of Henry Rogers in Plainfield for the purpose of organizing a religious society of the Universalist denomination. Amos Scott was chosen chairman and Isaac Woodworth, secretary. The next meeting was held March 18th, when it was voted that the society be known as the United Universalist Society of Bridgewater, Brookfield and Plainfield.

The present church was erected in 1835 and dedicated. A young man by the name of L. C. Brown was pastor of the society during the time of the church building and when it was dedicated he was ordained. He afterward became a very noted and eloquent minister of the Universalist denomination. Some of the most able men in the denomination filled the desk from time to time, including the Revs. Dr. Skinner, A. B. Grash, Dr. Thomas, J. Sawyer and others. When the dark cloud of the Civil War hovered over our country the Rev. Richard Coleman was pastor here. He preached a war sermon, as did most of his brother ministers, and it so disorganized the unity that for a time there were no regular services but up to 1865 occasional services were held, when the doors were closed.

In the summer of 1870 the Rev. Daniel Ballou came here canvassing for the Centenary fund and at this time urged the people here to repair the church. It was in the next summer, 1871, that the Rev. A. A. Thayer, agent for the *Christian Leader* came here in the interest of that paper. The old, delapidated church appealed to his denominational loyalty and he asked for an appointment to preach here. The following Sunday services were held in the Union church and in a business meeting which followed Mr. Thayer urged the people to repair the church. As a result, a committee of young men, consisting of Fred B. Foote, Lorin Scott and Orson Wolcott were chosen and they immediately went to work soliciting funds and by January next they had raised about $1200 and the needed repairs were made. The church was rededicated in February, 1873, Rev. A. J. Canfield, then of Utica, preaching the dedicating sermon. In the following March Rev. Luther Rice began his work and was succeeded sometime in the Seventies by Rev. LeGrande Powers. T. D. Cook was his successor and failing health obliging him to resign, Mrs. Powell of Herkimer filled the pulpit for a time, after which J. H. Stewart supplied for two years. H. O. Somers came here in the summer of 1887. The following spring the church was newly papered and stained glass windows put in. Charles Legal came the next winter from the Canton school and was succeeded by Rev. J. Murray Atwood. Rev. Charles Vail came next and preached two years. His successor was William N. Lawrence, who left here to take charge of the society in Utica. During the winter Mrs. Lawrence and Rev. E. W. Fuller alternately supplied the pulpit. Rev. Artemus L. Partridge was the next pastor and after his departure, Daniel Ballou filled the pulpit up to the time of his death. Rev. J. L. Dowson was then secured and during his pastorate the church was again extensively repaired and a new furnace installed. Rev. H. A. Abbott was his successor and following him came Rev. G. F. Babbitt, who left this church for a new field in Bristol. Rev. W. A. Render of Cicero was then called as the next pastor and he was followed by Rev. DeWitt Lampher. Mrs. Blanche Wright Morey of Newport is now very ably supplying the pulpit alternate weeks and is presenting to her congregations able and gifted discourses.

EPISCOPAL CHURCH

Christ church is one of the oldest Episcopal parishes in Oneida county. The parish was organized in October, 1839. A small chapel was the first place of worship but this at a later date was removed from its original foundation, which was located near the present Hibbard House, and placed on the site of the Baptist church, which had previously been destroyed by fire, and in addition to a new part, was used by this society together with the Methodists and Baptists and known as the Union church. Services were conducted here for many years until a new church building was erected on another street where services were conducted and the old building was given over to various forms of public entertainments, but repairs being neglected, it gradually fell into a state of decay and was rendered unsafe for use, and wearied and worn, seemingly, by years of steady service it stands a "superannuated" structure, mutely pleading for help.

The first rector in the little chapel was the Rev. Seth Davis, who had charge from 1839 to 1841. Mr. Davis was succeeded in 1841 by Rev. James Sunderland. Following his pastorate the pulpit was filled in succession by the following, who either acted as regular pastors or as lay readers, serving in many instances in conjunction with other parish charges: Rev. Fortune C. Brown (intermittently) 1842–1844, with occasional assistance from Rev. Nathan Burgess; Rev. David M. Fackler, 1845; Rev. William A. Matson, 1847 (connected with Grace church, Waterville); Rev. Thomas N. Benedict, 1849, who visited this parish only a few times. No regular services were held until 1853 when the Rev. E. W. Hagar of Clayville officiated once a month and the pulpit was vacant again until 1856 when occasional services were conducted by Dr. William T. Gibson of Waterville and Rev. J. E. Battin. In 1861 Rev. William J. Alger of Paris Hill held a few services and continued to hold monthly services until 1867. The following were then in charge: Rev. J. B. Wicks, 1871; Rev. M. L. Kern of Clayville, 1872; Rev. C. H. Gardner, 1874; Rev. Thomas Bell, 1875; Rev. George A. Chambers, 1876; Rev. J. B. Wicks, 1877–1881; Rev. Joel Davis, 1883–1886; Rev. B. E. Whipple, 1887–1888; Rev. W. B. Coleman, 1889; Rev. J. B. Avirett, 1893; Rev. E. B. Doolittle, 1894.

In 1895 the new edifice was erected under the supervision of Rev. E. B. Doolittle. This structure when completed presented an exceedingly fine and neat appearance, being furnished throughout with new and attractive furnishings. Rev. Mr. Hig-

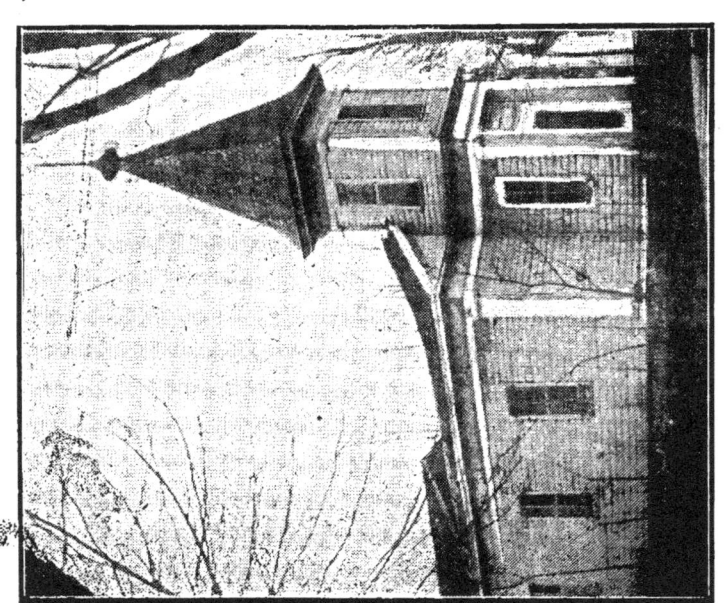

CHRIST EPISCOPAL CHURCH

OLD UNION CHURCH

gins was the next regular pastor. Rev. Mr. Evans of the Clay-ville church was the next officiating clergyman and from his departure until the present time the pulpit has been supplied at different times by lay readers who have rendered excellent service.

BAPTIST CHURCH

This church was constituted July 12, 1826, with sixteen members. Rev. Amasa Smith was the first pastor and labored here about nine years. He was succeeded by Rev. Jonathan P. Simmons in 1835 and among the other early pastors were Revs. Jason Corwin, Daniel Dye, P. W. Mills, D. W. Smith and J. H. Messenger. D. W. Smith at a later date took charge of the Female Seminary.

The first church built by this society stood upon the hill west of the village (near the old cemetery) and was erected in 1826. In 1840 it was removed nearer the center of the village and extensively repaired. About 1862 it was destroyed by fire. At that time the Baptists were not holding meetings in it, but it was occupied by the Methodists. The Episcopalians at the time were holding services in a small building owned by them which stood on the site of John Williams' residence and an agreement was made to move this to the Baptist ground, where all three denominations should conduct their meetings in it, and has since been known as the Union church. The Episcopalians were the last to hold services there but after they erected a new building the old one remained vacant, except for occasional town purposes, but is now in a state of decay.

FRATERNITIES AND SOCIETIES

WESTERN STAR LODGE NO. 15, F. & A. M.

Western Star Lodge is the oldest Masonic lodge in the county. It was chartered at the settlement known as Farwell's Hill, south of the village. Soon after the Lodge was instituted it built a hall, which now stands on the farm of Mrs. W. J. Scott and used as a tenant house. The lodge occupied this building until 1804 when it built the structure it now occupies but which was then located on South street on the site of the Cottage hotel !barn. Soon after the Perkins store burned (1857) the building was moved to the present location. About 1892 the hall was repaired and refurnished and during the process the book containing the records of the early years was lost.

During the years of agitation against Masonry, Western Star Lodge was one of the lodges that held meetings regularly. Lodges dropped out until the number, originally fifty-nine, became fifteen. It held together under difficulties and the loyal members were even forced to hold their meetings in the woods. During this period the Lodge was kept up by five men, Joshua Babcock, Thompson Holdridge, Samuel Richards, James Rhodes and Thomas Converse.

The history of the Lodge dates from April 21, 1796, when twelve members of the craft living in and near Bridgewater petitioned for a charter, asking also and obtaining the consent of Amicable lodge of Whitestown. The names of the petitioners, and their lodges as far as now known, are as follows: Ephraim Waldo, Amicable; Gurdon Thompson, Washington; Alexander Tackles, Temple, Vt.; Zadock Rider, Union; Robert Dixon, Pain; Levi Carpenter, Jr., Urial, Conn.; Thomas Brown, Joseph Farwell, Daniel Perkins, James Bolton, Isaac Mitchell and James Kinne.

In January of the following year the charter was granted

for the establishment of the new lodge, to be known as Western Star, and to be located at Bridgewater, in the town of Sangerfield, Herkimer county. It was not until May 18th of that year that the lodge actually commenced its independent life. On that date Jedidiah Sanger summoned the officers named in the warrant, together with the members of Amicable lodge, and in Amicable's rooms in Whitestown, duly installed the first officers of Western Star. Those officers were James Kinne, Worshipful Master; Thomas Brown, Senior Warden; and Daniel Perkins, Junior Warden. The first regular meeting was held at the residence of Ephraim Waldo, in Bridgewater, on June 1st, 1797, when the other officers of the lodge were elected, but who they were the record fails to show other than that Guerdon Thompson was Secretary. Thus the light of Western Star was kindled.

The first annual meeting was held December 7, 1797, and there were elected Thomas Brown, Worshipful Master; Daniel Perkins, Senior Warden; Levi Carpenter, Junior Warden; Charles Crosby, Secretary; and they were installed, so the record tells in quaint language, by James Kinne, Worshipful Master; Richard Sanger, Senior Warden; and George Halpin, Junior Warden; Amasa Andrews being present.

The old charter, written on parchment, was signed by Robert Livingston, Grand Master; Jacob Morton, Deputy Grand Master; James Scott, Senior Grand Warden; Dewitt Clinton, Junior Grand Warden; John Abrams, Grand Secretary. The charter is dated January 18, 1797. It is still in possession of the Lodge and is preserved among the relics, but the Lodge works under a duplicate, granted by the Grand Lodge as the old one had become so worn and it was desirable to preserve the document because of its historic value. Through those years when Masonry was under public displeasure and meetings had to be held in secrecy this charter was in the custody of Samuel Richards who had pockets made in his underclothing in which he carried it about on his person, not willing to leave it where it would not be under his personal protection.

The Lodge also has a Bible, dated 1793, four years before the Lodge was instituted. This, too, has passed through the vicissitudes of age and persecution. It bears the imprint of Mark & Charles Kerr, Edinburgh, His Majesty's Printers.

The Lodge room contains several portraits of historic interest. One is that of Robert R. Livingston and is marked ''In Memory of Frederick Peirce, Pioneer in Bridgewater, and in Western Star, Given by F. P. Peirce.'' The other portraits are those of Samuel Richards, William Greenman, Hon. Alvah Penny, Samuel Button and W. J. Beal.

The influence of Western Star Lodge upon Bridgewater and surrounding community has been recognized for many years. It has done much to promote the lofty teachings and principles of the order and incorporate them into the life of the people.

Its jurisdiction includes the village of Bridgewater, Unadilla Forks, Leonardsville and Brookfield.

A fair was held in 1908 which placed the society upon a firm financial basis and is now in a prosperous condition and contains in its membership many men of prominence in the outside world.

The present officers are: William E. Owens, Worshipful Master; Adon P. Brown, Senior Warden; Howard C. Miller, Junior Warden; Aaron Mather, Treasurer; Henry C. Sorn, Secretary; Leslie P. Curtis, Chaplain; Frank J. Southworth, Senior Deacon; Leland W. Livermore, Junior Deacon; Chester Clark, Senior Master of Ceremonies; Homer Hackley, Junior Master of Ceremonies; George W. Bailey, Tiler; Merton C. Rogers, Marshal; John S. Wheeler, Organist; Trustees, W. J. Beal*, C. H. Clark, W. H. Rowland.

One of the prominent members whose memory is revered was James Avery Rhodes of Babcock Hill. In his declining years when about ninety years of age he wrote two letters to the Lodge which have been preserved and framed and occupy a place in the Lodge room. Their message meant much to the members of the order and are reproduced here; as follows:

* Deceased.

Babcock Hill, N. Y., December 26, 1883.
Brothers of Western Star Lodge, No. 15
    I received notice of attendance from your respected secretary. In my advanced old age I can not with propriety attend evening sessions. Sixty-five years ago and many years after I have seen your hall

filled with the most respected part of the community from all the surrounding towns. Many a time and oft have I met them there when friendship and brotherly love filled every heart and the dominant emulation was: "Who can best work and who can best agree." My time is, of course, short. I hope the Supreme Architect, whose Temple is all space, whose altar is earth, sea and skies, will enable me through Him who went on High to prepare a place for us to lay hold on the stars and bid the world pass on. There is no institution in the world that can show so clean a record as yours. Long may it wave is the wish of your humble servant and brother,

J. A. RHODES.

Babcock Hill, N. Y., Dec. 15, 1885.

Brethren of Western Star Lodge:

Our worthy brother, John W. Collins, is no more. He was made a Mason in our lodge in 1822, subsequently of the Chapter, and had his residence in Toledo, Ohio, and a prominent member throughout. The above occurrence reminds me of my membership in 1819. I was then permitted to enter the portals of your lodge. There I saw a worthy representation from the four adjoining counties, Oneida, Madison, Otsego and Herkimer, the Judiciary, the Medical, the Military and the Colonial. Also the church from the oldest St. Peter's to the youngest Noncombatant Quaker. The Lodge was presided over by that old Masonic Patriarch, Israel Brewer. Well do I remember his charge to me as a member of Western Star Lodge to be cautious over all my words and actions and as a Mason to walk upright before God and man.

There I saw in place among other things the warrant dated January 18, 1797, by which the Lodge was organized. There I saw the name in signature of the Hon. Robert R. Livingston, the companion and associate of Washington, Franklin, Adams, Hancock, Warren and others, whose names will live in history when the builders of the cloud-capped towers of the old world will be forgotten.

Being now in my ninety-sixth year, my trembling knees and palpitating heart warn me that my sands are nearly out of the hour glass and hope my Masonic Brothers will smooth the turf under which they are invited to deposit my remains in the Bridgewater cemetery at a proper time. Farewell, Brothers.

J. AVERY RHODES.

KISMET CHAPTER, O. E. S.

Kismet Chapter, No. 217, O. E. S., was organized April 27, 1901, by Mrs. Betsy M. Ballou, District Deputy Grand Matron, of the Twelfth Eastern Star District, with a full staff of officers from Ivy Chapter, No. 65, of Utica, N. Y.

There were fifteen charter members with Carolyn R. Terry, Worthy Matron, and William J. Beal, Worthy Patron.

Western Star Lodge, No. 15, F. & A. M. gave the sisters the use of their hall, thus beginning a long list of kindnesses shown the young sisterhood.

A charter was granted by the Grand Chapter of the State of New York October 10, 1901, and the Chapter was constituted by Mrs. Ella L. F. Nicholson, District Deputy Grand Matron, October 31, 1901.

During this year seven members were initiated, making a membership of twenty-two. The next year two members were added.

In December new officers were elected with Mrs. Maud R. Peirce as Worthy Matron and Franklin J. Southworth, Worthy Patron. The next year only one member was added.

During the fourth and fifth years several members removed to other localities, little interest was shown, and the outlook was a gloomy one. Only by the faithfulness of a few was the charter saved.

After careful consideration it was decided that Kismet Chapter rent their present rooms over Rising's store and to change the place and hour of meeting to enable them to meet at the same hour that Western Star Lodge held their meetings. The result was all that could be desired. Kismet Chapter began to grow rapidly. One hundred and thirty persons have been members of the Chapter, of whom eighty-six are still members.

In February, 1908 eleven members withdrew and on March 10 Winfield Chapter was organized by them as charter members.

The first officers have been: Worthy Matrons, Carolyn R. Terry, Maud R. Peirce, Kittie E. Beal, Kate L. Woodworth, Ellen A. Moses, Phoebe D. Hoxie, Anna D. Matteson, Alida B. Randall; Worthy Patrons, W. J. Beal, F. J. Southworth, T. D. Carter. W. H. Jones, Andrew McCarthy, Brother Beal serving six of the nearly nine years of their existence. The Chapter is in a flourishing condition with a good outlook for the future.

UNADILLA VALLEY GRANGE

Unadilla Valley Grange, No. 1152, was organized December 22, 1908, with thirty members. C. H. Clark, who is called the father of the Grange, was the first Master. He occupied the chair two years. He was succeeded by Myron Brown, Homer Hackley, W. H. Jones and Harold Fitch, who has been re-elected for the year 1915. The Lecturers for this time were Mattie Hackley, Minnie Stevens, Jane Langworthy, Anna Walsh, Evelyn Whitmore and Elizabeth Scott. The fifth anniversary was celebrated with a very enjoyable banquet. It has at present 100 members. A site has been given for a hall by I. E. Stevens and $1500 subscribed to build the same. The Grange rooms are now located on the upper floor of the Doolittle block. State Master Godfrey has paid it a visit. It must be counted among the valuable assets in the community, contributing socially, educationally and profitably.

WOMAN'S ART CLUB

The Woman's Art Club of Bridgewater was organized in January, 1881, and its work has ever since gone on without interruption.

It is believed to be the oldest society of its kind in this section of the State. At its beginning six ladies, who had been taking painting lessons of Miss Ella M. Gardner, agreed when their teacher left them to go on with their work and to meet at stated intervals to criticize and help each other. Each member was allowed to bring a friend to the meetings and usually had some form of literary entertainment, an essay or sketch of an artist or his work and always an enjoyable time socially and the membership gradually increased. Their name was then "Salmagundi." A president and vice-president were elected annually, Mrs. Emily P. Peirce serving as president the first five years.

With the larger membership the social character of the club developed rapidly and the membership increased to thirty-five.

In 1886 rules and regulations were adopted and the name changed to The Woman's Art Club and began to study, using DeForest's Short History of Art as a text book. With the aid of books and illustrated magazines the foundation of a knowledge of the world's greatest artists was laid.

In 1891, when the *History of Art* was finished, the membership had fallen to eighteen. They then began to study the history of European countries with their literature and art. Rome came first, and their authority was principally Hare's *Walks in Rome*. Afterward in the following order they studied in the same way, Florence, Venice, Holland, Germany, England, . Spain and France.

On October 17, 1896, it was voted to become a registered club in the Extension Department of the University of the State of New York. Since then they have had a Traveling Library. The first years they had twenty-five books. For the years since 1900 they have had fifty or seventy-five books on . the subject each year.

The present Constitution and By-Laws were adopted August 25, 1899.

In October, 1902, they began the history of United States from the earliest times, and continued to study our country till 1908. Since then we have visited by book Mexico, Japan, China, Russia and India. We are now taking a three years course on the State of New York. In 1908 they visited by book Mexico and this year they are visiting Japan and its wonderful people.

The number is limited to twenty-five and now have a membership of twenty-five with one honorary member. Several names are being considered by the membership committee.

The meetings are held once in every month at the homes of the members, each taking their turn in alphabetical order in entertaining the club, conducting the lesson and doing other necessary work. The officers are elected annually; the present executive board are President, Miss Grace E. Brown; First Vice-President, Mrs. Anna F. Rising; Second Vice-President, Miss Lelia B. Palmer; Corresponding Secretary and Treasurer, Miss Elizabeth Penney; Librarian, Mrs. Minnie Stevens.

They celebrated our first, fifth, tenth, twentieth, twenty-fifth and thirtieth anniversaries by holding receptions and banquets.

July 25, 1913, the Club met with Mrs. Emily Peirce when the six original members were together for the last time. In less than two weeks their hostess and first president had passed away. Nine names are now listed "In Memoriam."

In the earliest days of the club and when they were struggling for existence and recognition their efforts were ridiculed and motives misunderstood. At this time a feeling of mutual helpfulness and benefit was established among them and the recollection of those early days has bound them closely together as they earnestly endeavor to be a means of culture for themselves and to be an inspiration to those about them. It is remarkable the perfect harmony that has existed among the members. So deep an interest is felt in the work of the club that no matter how intense the heat of summer, the impassibility of the highways, or the fierce storms of winter, the ladies may be seen on their way to attend the meetings some of whom must travel each time several times to the gathering place. Qualities of patience and perseverence flourish among them and however much they may delight in recalling the past they are looking forward to the future, trying to make the most of their opportunities and to leave on record their efforts for the advancement of womankind.

BRIDGEWATER UNION SCHOOL

SCHOOLS

'Tis education forms the common mind;
Just as the twig is bent, the tree's inclined.

The pioneers realized the great importance of educational advantages and appreciated the blessings derived from an enlightened mind. They did not need a compulsory education law to impress it upon their attention that the young must be trained and prepared to take their places in the world. Amid the toils of a backwoodsman's life and in the midst of many deprivations this need was ever in mind and as soon as a footing had been secured in their new home they set earnestly to work to establish institutions of learning. True it is that they were rude structures, hewed as it were from the forest itself, and the youth of that day had no comforts of warmth or ready conveniences at their command. Often they were obliged to travel miles to reach the school in all kinds of weather but such experiences as these was the common lot of their time and such obstacles were only means of developing in them that vigorous, hardy spirit that conquered all difficulties with which they met. The school children of today little realize or can appreciate their privileges or great advantages unless they have instilled into their minds the mighty sacrifices that were necessary before such improvements could be accomplished.

Schools were taught early in the Farwell neighborhood but they were few and scattering. About 1796–1797 a log school house was built a mile north of North Bridgewater. The building known as "the old red school house" was destroyed by fire in 1855. This was located on the site of the wood colored house near Edward McDermott's farm. In the fall of the same year school was opened in the building which was formerly C. O. Palmer's wagon shop and was then situated in the corner of the Langworthy lot. Mrs. Mary Wilkes and Miss Maria Sheldon were the teachers. School was held here until the following spring when a new building was erected on the site of the old one. Anna S. Hall was the first teacher. At times the capacity was not large enough to accommodate the great number of pupils and as there was only one teacher a division was made and a primary department was held in the upper rooms of the Peirce tenant house by the creek, the building now occupied by George Tripp. The school south of the village continued in that service until 1881.

An academy was established at Bridgewater village in 1826 and discontinued in 1839. This building was located between the residence of Dr. Whitford and the creek. A part of the same building is still standing and helps to form Dr. Whitford's barn and another part was used in the construction of the present Doolittle block. During the first years of the existence of this academy it was very prosperous and had an average attendance of one hundred pupils. A building, 58x36 feet, was erected at a cost of $2500 and was built of heavy hewed timbers. There were three floors above the stone and brick basement, which contained two huge brick ovens. This school contained a good chemical apparatus and it also maintained a library. After discontinuing this academy it was used as a select school. Much of it had fallen into decay by 1842 and one room was used at that time for a store by Delos and Samuel DeWolf until the building was bought by Dr. Whitford and disposed of in the manner mentioned above.

Another school known as the Bridgewater Seminary was established in December, 1847, and in May, 1849, its name was changed to the ''Bridgewater Female Seminary.'' The depart- ment of music had a high reputation and many attended. This school in 1851 was under the supervision of Rev. D. W. Smith, a former pastor of the Baptist church. This school was very prosperous and had a large attendance but finally declined and at length was discontinued. The building used for this semi- nary is now used as a residence and stands at the head of the street known as ''the Lane.''

The school south of the village was continued as a common school until 1881 when it was voted to make it a Union School and a tax of $2000 was ordered to be raised for the new build- ing. This structure was erected in 1882 and continued as a Union school until the principalship of J. B. Swinney in the year 1901 when by his earnest and strenuous efforts it was raised to the standing of a high school and brought to a flourishing condition. This was continued as a high school until 1908 when the standard was again lowered to that of a union school. Following is the list of principals: L. D. Browne, 1882–1884; George A. Knapp, 1884–1885; J. K. Barclay, 1885–1886; Mr. Severance, 1886–1887; F. M. Westfall, 1887–1889; W. L. Avery, 1889–1891; S. D. Butler, 1892–January, 1897; William D. Morrow, spring of 1897–fall of 1898; A. L. Smith, 1899–March, 1901; J. B. Swinney, March, 1901–1902; A. A. Upham, 1902–1903; F. J. Salter, 1903–1906; Luther Moses, 1906–1907; C. H. Jones, 1907–1909; R. B. Graves, 1909–1911; H. L. Gillis, 1911–1913; Earle Stanley Lougee, 1913–

Principal Lougee is to be highly commended on the splendid service he has rendered the school in bringing it up to the present high standard of excellency.

The present Board of Education consists of the following members: President, L. P. Curtis; Clerk, H. C. Rogers; William Pritchard, Irving Stevens, John Walsh.

STAGE COACH DAYS

"Yoho! past streams, in which the cattle cool their feet and where the rushes grow; past farms and rickyards; past last year's stacks, cut slice by slice away, and showing in the waning light like ruined gables, old and brown. Yoho! Yoho! through ditch and brake, upon the plowed land and the smooth, along the steep hillside and steeper wall, as if it were a phantom hunter. Clouds, too! And a mist upon the hollow! Yoho! Why, now we travel like the moon herself; hiding this minute in a grove of trees; next minute in a patch of vapor; emerging now upon our broad, clear course; withdrawing now, but always dashing on—our journey is a counterpart of hers. Yoho! A match against the moon. Yoho! Yoho!"—Dickens.

In the days when the great stagecoach rattled along our highways Bridgewater was a very important center and it is indeed hard to imagine that it was a far more important commercial center than Utica. People came here from many miles around to trade. The Cherry Valley turnpike was a great transportation highway between Albany and Syracuse and most of the traffic between these points went through here. Also it was the direct stage route between Utica and New Berlin and the lines intersected here, making it a transfer point.

Stories of the old stage days are numerous. There was the same bustle and excitement, and even more so, when the covered, four-horse coaches, containing sometimes as many as twenty passengers, arrived and left than there is now at our railroad stations. The tooting horn announced the stage's near approach and all was hurry and excitement. One or two incidents will reflect something of the manner of the drivers and the stage coaches of those days. Usually when the great top-heavy coach was loaded and everybody was packed in, the driver came out with a great flourish, gave a leap to the seat and with a snap of his lashed whip and a yell the horses moved off with a jump. This was all a part of the procedure and the stage driver who lacked any of this enthusiasm was not considered fit for the job. On one occasion it is related, which was one of similar occasions, the driver gave a yell too soon, or at least had not got hold of the reins and the horses, darting forward, made the turn to go north to Utica and turned too short and the stage toppled over. It was loaded inside and out to its full capacity and many were injured. They were mostly Quakers from the West, who had been in attendance at a great meeting of Quakers at Morris. On another occasion the stage started up so quickly as to precipitate a man who was sitting back of the driver. He fell over backward, striking the ground on his head and shoulders and sustained injuries from which he died.

It is hard to convey to the people of this generation anything of the activity along the Cherry Valley turnpike. Men who are now living relate that when boys they sat on the steps of their homes and saw droves of cattle, horses and sheep pass by for many hours. Until 1843 all stock for Eastern markets was driven over this turnpike to Albany. After that date stock was usually transported over the New York Central. Every tavern had its stock yard located where the stock was fed and cared for in every way. Eighteen stage horses were kept standing in Bridgewater barns all the time for substitutes when other stage horses had traveled their limited stretch. Taverns were numerous about Bridgewater. The highway which is now a state road north to Utica and which extends south to New Berlin was known as the old Utica-Bridgewater Plank Road Company and for many years was planked. When the new state road was constructed north of the village several of these planks were unearthed. Most goods roads were private enterprises at that time and the toll gates, which still remain a memory to many of this time, were then an established institution. One was located at North Bridgewater where the railroad crosses the highway; another just south of the village, just below the farm of Giles Scott; one near West Winfield and another west of the town near the Bellfield district. These toll gates were stationed at all entrances of the town. The toll was about four cents per horse, six cents for one horse and carriage, a shilling a pair, two cents for sheep, two cents for horseback rider and some commutation to regular patrons who lived in the vicinity. It is related that back in the early days, as well as later days of the toll system, that now and then travelers delighted in beating the toll gate keepers. A frequent method used was to pass through and promise to pay when returning and the traveler took occasion to come back by some other way.

Stories are also told where drivers have rushed at break-neck speed through the gate, pulling on the reins with all their strength, seemingly attempting to pull the horse to a standstill. The harder the driver pulled the faster the horse ran for he had been trained to do so.

Taverns were located all along the route and were important factors in the life of the day. The Harrison Briggs house which burned a few years ago was formerly a hotel and kept by Moses Ward. When the Center church was in existence the people came for all day services and before the church was heated, the people were accustomed to seek the warmth and glow of this tavern fireside and replenish their foot stoves for the further services of the day. The Tuckerman house was also a tavern. The Rising store was originally a tavern and the old original floor is still in the building underneath the upper floor. The house where Eugene True now resides was at one time a tavern but at a later date the structure was lowered and made into a private residence. The old hotel which stands by Byron Murray's on Hackley street was at one time located on the road to West Winfield, west of Frank Murray's present farm.

BUILDINGS

The brick building where E. M. & H. O. Rising are located was originally used for a hotel. It was continued for some time for that purpose and then transformed into a store by Deloss DeWolfe in 1843. He was followed in the business by the partners, Russell & Mott, and they were succeeded by Samuel DeWolfe. William Greenman was the next merchant and the business has been conducted in succession by the following: Henry Robinson, Williams & Bort, W. H. Greenman, George Greenman, Rising Bros. and E. M. & H. O. Rising.

The store which stood on the site of the present Masonic building was destroyed by fire in 1857, as were also the adjoining buildings to the right. A. M. Perkins occupied the place at the time and after the fire he opened a store in the building which is now the Cottage hotel. Frank Malloy at one time conducted a hardware store here. This was sold about 1868 to J. C. Folts, who conducted a store here. It was used for this purpose for several years but was finally sold and transformed into a hotel In 1864 the Masonic building, which was located on South street on the site of the Cottage hotel barn, was moved to the place where the Perkins store was burned and C. W. Stoddard opened the lower part as a general store and the upper rooms were used by the lodge. Th remaining vacant lot was then rebuilt and Isaac Woodworth opened a grocery store on the corner. Fred Utter and Samuel Griffin also conducted business here. This was occupied later by James Howe for a hardware store and now contains the Helmer Undertaking rooms. C. W. Stoddard continued in business for twenty-eight years and then sold to H. C. Rogers. A small building at the right of this store was at one time used for a boot manufactory and conducted by Lyman Strictland. Here were employed quite a number of workmen and boots were made and shipped in barrels to Chicago.

The original store, which formed the rear part of W. H. Rowland's store was at one time used for a shoe shop. After serving this purpose Alfred Bliven opened it as a store and finally sold to the partners Marsh & Turner. Their successors have been: I. D. Peckham, W. C. Marsh, T. D. Carter, Beals & Rowland and W. H. Rowland. This building, together with the meat market adjoining and the Cottage Hotel barn was destroyed by fire in September, 1913.

In the early Fifties B. F. Rindge kept hotel in the building which was on the site of the present Doolittle Block. He was followed by John Bowker. In 1857 the building was burned and Mr. Bowker moved to the building now the Hibbard House, which was built by Levi Bostwick about 1812 and he was the landlord for a number of years. A brick building opposite was built for a hotel by Harvey Curtis, who kept it many years. It was at one time known as the Beebe House, but has been called by the present name since A. C. Hibbard was the proprietor. The building has been enlarged from time to time and in various way improved.

About 1867 Alfred Bliven moved part of the old Academy on the corner opposite the Hibbard House, where the hotel had previously burned and after enlarging it, opened a hotel. William Wilson was at one time proprietor and from him derived the name of the Wilson House. It was used for a hotel for some time and then remained vacant. It was finally sold to a Mr. Doolittle of Utica and has since been known as the Doolittle Block and has been put to the various uses of stores, apartments and entertainment halls.

The building which was formerly used by C. O. Palmer as a shop was at one time a distillery and the livery stable near was for many years used both for a tannery and a boot manufactory. It was then changed to a cheese factory and conducted for many years by Zenas Eldred and has since been used for a livery barn.

At one time a cooper's shop was located between the residences of E. M. Rising and M. D. Willis. Thomas Parkinson, father of T. W. Parkinson, once conducted a tailoring establishment in the old brick store and employed several hands.

A wagon shop was located at one time on the site of the R. J. Wilkinson house. This was later finished off by Jacob Spring and the front part was used as a dwelling and the rear section served as a blacksmith shop. Mr. Spring sold this building to Heman Seifert and he in turn sold to R. J. Wilkinson. This building was destroyed by fire and Mr. Wilkinson soon erected a new house and a shop was also built a short distance away.

The building known as the "Broker" Jones shop, which stood on the west side of the creek near Dr. Whitford's, was built by Prentiss Brown for a blacksmith shop. Later George Latus conducted a blacksmith shop here and lived in the Porter house. This building stood for a great many years in a delapidated condition and was helped to its ruin one celebration night when several men and boys of the town fastened ropes around it and lowered it to the ground.

DESCENDANTS OF EARLY SETTLERS

The following is a collection of short sketches of the descendants of the early settlers of Bridgewater. The lack of uniformity of style is due to the fact that these outlines and sketches were gathered from different sources and prepared by several individuals. The various notes give an idea of these family representatives down to the presnt day.

IVES FAMILY

Joel Ives married Annie Goodwin from Connecticut. They had three children, Julia, Joel and Lucy. Julia married Marvin Scott. Their six children were Joel, Cornelia, Giles, Julia, Willard and Emily.

Willard married Emeline Munn. Three children were born to them, of whom only one daughter, Lizzie, who married Dr. Ward, is living and has three daughters, Annah, Margaret and Cornelia.

Giles married Elizabeth Babcock. They had two sons, Irving and Lorin.

Lorin married Clara Ferris of Auburn. They have six children, Giles, Fred, Charles, Earl, Irving and Elizabeth. Giles married Harriet Palmer and they have four children, Palmer, Willard, Hosmer and Helen. Charles married Minnie Davis and they have one daughter, Marian Lucy. Irving married Beth Hartshorn of Hamilton and they have one son, Reginald Hartshorn.

Emily married John Tuckerman. They have two children, Bertha and George.

Joel, the son of Joel Ives died after his marriage and the other daughter, Lucy, married Benjamin Maxon (a Sabbatarian). They had two children, Sofia and Rufus and lived in Jefferson county. Joel Ives' widow (Annie Goodwin) married for her second husband, Epaphroditus Foote. (This line of descent can be traced through the Foote family on another page.)

WALDO FAMILY

Ephraim Waldo had five sons and four daughters. Two

sons died in childhood. Caroline married Alvin Blackman: she and her two children died. Her husband, Alvin Blackman afterward married Harriet Waldo; no children were born to them. Sarah married W. W. Blackman; one son and one daughter were born to them, both of whom are living at present, Mrs. Bailey and Dr. W. W. Blackman. Dimmick married Orrisa Johnston Clark; one son and two daughters were born to them, all of whom are dead. Wellington never married; he is now dead. Eunice married Thomas Parkinson; two sons were born to them, one of whom survives, T. W. Parkinson. Alvin, the youngest, never married; he is still living. T. W. Parkinson has two sons, Clarence and Floyd. Clarency married S. Belle Rowsan and they have two children, Clarence and Thomas. Floyd married Clara N. Hess.

PEIRCE FAMILY

Not long ago a man noted for his literature and oratory ended a cross-country outing at Bridgewater. At least there is ground for the belief that he considered his journey happily ended with a brief stay there, for afterward, at the close of one of his most charming lectures he described his wanderings and the old village and its people, drawing for his hearers a fascinating word-picture of the winding, willow-fringed river, the name of which, Unadilla, and the attractiveness which it suggested to him, he declared well fitted it to become the appellation of a girl.

Others, too, have been drawn to this pleasant country, and like him, have found within its boundaries their ideal. One such set out in the year 1796 from Stonington, Connecticut. Six feet, two and one-half inches tall, carrying with ease on his broad shoulders the necessary accoutrements for the journey and his stay, he found little difficulty in making his way on foot along the Hudson and Mohawk and into the wilderness of the "Chenango Twenty Towns laid out on the Unadilla River." There his orderly mind, restrained by Quaker discipline and developed by a training in one of the learned professions, caused him to discern the free outlook which his ambition sought and led him to become one of Bridgewater's pioneers. That man was Frederick Peirce.

Like all settlers he "took up land." The plot was near the "Center." At once, single handed, he proceeded with characteristic vigor and thoroughness to clear a field and sow it with wheat and to erect the inevitable log house. This building, one of the first in town, stood on the east side of what is now the "State Road" about three hundred feet south-east of the Chapin homestead of today, on a site about a hundred feet back from the highway.

Twice again this stalwart pioneer covered the ground between Bridgewater and Stonington, once at the end of the first summer and again in the following spring. The latter trip, like both of the others, was on foot, but on this occasion it was at the side of the horse bearing Mary Oaks, his bride, and all of their worldly goods.

Little is known of the life of this worthy couple in their new log cabin home. Certain it is that hard work and homely fare soon brought all the comforts then deemed necessary and proper. The story of a single event, however, survives. It is to the effect that on a certain occasion the family's only cow strayed from her usual grazing ground and that before she had been found roaming the forest-covered East Street neighborhood, a large black bear was encountered by the searcher. Bruin was near the trout brook so well known to modern fishermen, and was inclined to dispute the crossing. In driving off the prowler and in finally discovering the whereabouts of the cow valuable assistance is said to have been rendered by a dog named Bose whose general good qualities were so unusual as to almost make it seem that an injustice has been done in not bestowing the name on others of his tribe to this day, as a memorial of his fine qualities. The whole incident seems to have been devoid of disaster, yet it must have been fraught with elements of great importance, else why should it have been preserved and its frequent recital received with awe by each generation, even to the fourth!

After a time the family removed to North Bridgewater, no great distance, indeed, but to more comfortable quarters and among more numerous neighbors. The house occupied stood nearly opposite the present site of the Hotel, and a portion of it now forms a part of the Albert Parkhurst residence. Here, again, the family's life developed little which then or now could be of public interest, and this record may be closed after noting a few matters indicative of its member's sterling characteristics.

Primarily, Frederick Peirce was a farmer. Education had fitted him to take a high place in the profession which is now known as engineering, but which in that early day found little opportunity outside of the military camp or the occasional work of the land surveyor. To him, therefore, naturally was intrusted the task of planing the system of highways required for the development of the new town, and the records in the Clerk's office show that nearly all in use today are the result of his careful study. To his lasting credit, it should be noted, that some of the hilliest and least used do not form a part of his work.

With the assistance of five daughters and two sons, the family long and diligently endeavored to introduce into Bridgewater the culture of silk. In this they achieved a degree of success, but its value consisted more in demonstrating the fact that the severe winters made the growing of the indispensible mulberry trees too uncertain to make the industry a paying one. The undertaking was kept up, however, until the ladies of the family were well supplied with silk garments produced, dyed, spun and woven by themselves. To such achievement they added the then common ones of supplying the woolen, linen and leather necessary for the whole family. A neighboring hatter worked the raw wool into felt hats and the itinerant shoe maker made the year's supply of boots and shoes, the material for all coming from their own farm. In fact, at one time apparently everything needed for their comfort and convenience, except iron and glass, was the result of the well directed and united efforts of the family applied to their own acres. Such frugality and industry tended in no wise to narrow the minds or shorten the mental vision of these worthy Connecticut Yankees or their descendants.

Frederick Peirce was in no sense a politician, and rarely an office holder, yet he was as active and keen in his patriotism as he might have been had the opportunity and his adherence to

Quaker principles allow him a place in his grandfather, Capt. Benjamin Peirce's company at Bunker Hill. He was a Free Mason, made such when Washington directed the policy of the order. His handwriting in the now lost book of records of Western Star Lodge, at one time and another read and identified by members of his family, show him to have been in frequent attendance at meetings in the early days.

One daughter and one son continued to live in Bridgewater. Guided in youth by probity and austerity they allowed no deviation therefrom in after life.

The daughter, Maria Peirce, was to a ripe old age a nurse, well trained in the practical school of that day, and many there are now living, who treasure with affection the memory of her soothing and healing ministrations.

The son, Nehemiah Nathaniel Peirce, popularly known as "the Colonel" on account of his military services as such, followed the example of his father both as to education and general business pursuits, departing therefrom only when for a brief time he was most successfully in charge of the sales department of the old Millard farm implement factory at Clayville.

In politics he was steadfastly Republican. Loyalty to the organization invariably led him to support its candidates, the only exception being in favor of his boyhood and lifelong friend William Croft Ruger, the Bridgewater lawyer who became a Chief Judge of our Court of Appeals. On many occasions he was chosen by the electorate to responsible office. Once he represented his district in the Assembly and in recognition of his services there was formally honored by receiving the "freedom of the City" of Utica. It is probable that he might have been sent to the Senate had he not declined the choice of the convention, a nomination by which was then equivalent to an election.

To him unquestionably belongs the credit of securing for his town its first railroad. As the result of his unaided effort the preliminary work which was followed by the construction of the railroad down the Unadilla Valley to New Berlin, was carried on, in recognition of which he was selected to turn the first spadeful of earth when the work thereon was finally begun.

In early manhood only did he live on a farm.   There he was one of the first, if not actually the first, to engage in hop culture, in Bridgewater.   Of this beginning it is needless to say more than that it surely lead to the development of a vast industry which was the means of bringing great wealth and a maximum population to the town.   His cheese factory was the first of its kind in his part of the State.   It must not be understood that cheese was not made in Bridgewater before his factory was established, rather that he was the first to produce it by such method, an example soon and widely followed.

Brick making also claimed his attention.   So long as material was available his plant was in operation, furnishing employment to many laborers.

It was always a source of pride for him to relate that he numbered among his friends the neighbor who invented and first manufactured the revolving horse-rake, that unique labor-saving farm implement which to this day is used in its original form in every civilized country.   The probable effect on the town had the inventor patented his idea and confined manufacture to his home locality was always a source of speculation, to which he sometimes added the possibilities which might arise from a test development of the coal discovered in the east hills.

In 1860 he married Emily Pullman, of Norway, this State.   This lady brought to his home and community all the practices and customs of the Hugenots, Americanized through two centuries at New Rochelle and New Paltz.   To these traits were abundantly added a culture and capability for broadening and better influences entrusted to few, and that she strove untiringly to use these gifts for the good of others is amply testified in many ways.   Two examples only, may be noted, each typical in its way of her ideal of neighborhood life.

Joining with her a half dozen ladies of kindred aims the "Art Club" was formed.   This organization is too well known to require any description here, the fact that the purposes of its founders has continued to be realized through so many years that among women's clubs it now has no senior, sufficiently indicating its worth.

To some there comes the opportunity and inclination to build hospitals or churches, libraries or halls, or to create foundations for widespread good or the perpetuation of a name. Denied the means of such achievements, this woman, at seventy-five years of age, availed herself of an opportunity as she saw it, by establishing a nursery in which she raised from seeds planted by herself, ornamental trees for free distribution, expecting no reward save the satisfaction which came from the desire to beauty and render more attractive the community in which she had spent the best of her life and effort. Already some hundreds of these trees have filled barren stretches and are promising the charm of shaded streets and lawns.

Such lives as these here mentioned, the living of which comprehend a century and more, have helped to make Bridgewater's history. There can be no doubt that they contributed to the alluring qualities of people and place which the lecturer found and described, and certain it is that their influence has not yet ceased.

Frederick P. Peirce of New York is the only son of Nehemiah N. Peirce. He married Maud Ross of Bridgewater and they have one daughter, Helen.

SOUTHWORTH FAMILY

Rev. James Southworth, tenth generation from the Plymouth ancestors, was born January 30th, 1769 and settled in Bridgewater in 1803. He organized the first church in the town and preached there twenty-three years and also preached at Paris Hill, Plainfield and Burlington. He had ten children, three of whom settled near Bridgewater, Dennison, John and Henry. James Southworth died at Bridgewater in 1826. John, born July 6th, 1797, married Harriet Hunt of Bridgewater. He died in April, 1869. Franklyn Southworth (son of Marcus, fourth son of John) lives on the old homestead. John had nine children of whom Normandie was the eldest. Normandie left Bridgewater at the age of 27 years.

William Newell, second son of John, was born September 16th, 1823. He was supervisor of the town for several years, and was a staunch Democrat. Mr. Southworth was a man of keen intellect and posted on all the subjects of the day. A niece of his tells as a little incident which came to her mind of distinctly remembering watching her uncle and Nathaniel

Tompkins play back gammon seventy-four games in succession
and when they stopped to eat supper she hid the board. Mr.
Southworth never married. He died at the old homestead
February 26, 1899. In this book will be found a sketch of the
Center church, containing most interesting history and written
in his natural style.

BROCKWAY FAMILY

Mr. and Mrs. Albert Brockway, grandparents of Mr. Albert
Parkhurst of North Bridgewater, were early settlers at that
place. On the occasion of their Golden Wedding anniversary
July 6th, 1876, a few facts appeared relative to the Brockway
family and is contained in the following interesting sketch:

"Mr. Albert Brockway, when a boy of sixteen, shouldered
his pack containing his all in the town of Saybrook, Connecticut
and came on foot and alone to Bridgewater where he has ever
since made his permanent home. Here he settled among the
pioneers of the town and probably no person now living in town
is better or more personally acquainted with its earliest history.

"Almost every farmer in this county and state feels interested in the welfare of Mr. Brockway as he has been one of the
most useful inventors of our county. By his mechanical quali-
fications all are being benefitted more than himself, as he never
had the benefit of a patent. Farmers, stop and think while you
are gathering your new-mown hay with Brockway's revolving
hay-rake, that he is an old man of eighty, still able to manufacture with his own hands, one of the simplest and most useful
implements in your occupation. Perhaps Bridgewater can't
boast of a greater merchanic than he has been and is at the
present writing. He still retains all of his power of mechanical
genius."

Albert Brockway died in March, 1885, aged 88 years.

Mrs. Henry Robinson (youngest daughter of Albert Brockway) and her husband now own and occupy the old Brockway
homestead place, known as Brockway's saw mill.

PALMER FAMILY

The Palmer family has been identified with the town of
Bridgewater from its first inception. Among its very earliest

settlers were Elias Palmer and wife Keturah Randall who came to his country by ox-team from Stonington, Conn. Their children were ten in number, two of whom remained in Bridgewater: George W. who married Belinda Loomis, their children being Lelia B. and Nettie A. Later in life Mr. Palmer married Lucy Guller who now resides in North Bridgewater with Lelia B. Palmer. Nettie A. married Hosea W. Palmer and now resides in Chicago. The youngest of these ten children was Lorenia A. who married C. Orlando Palmer, their children being Herbert E. and Jennie F. Herbert E. married Rosamond Brown, their only child being Ruth L., at present a teacher in Palmyra High School. Later Mr. Palmer married Alice V. Mather with whom he now lives in the village of Bridgewater. Jennie F. married Frank S. Tower and now resides in Geneva, N. Y.

Herbert E. Palmer is a figure well known to all in and about the town of Bridgewater. Joining the Masonic Fraternity early in life he has been exceptionally honored by the order, having been a Master of Western Star many terms, and later elected by the Grand Lodge District Deputy Grand Master for the 26th Masonic district. Mr. Palmer is an active Democrat and has served as postmaster under Cleveland, has been supervisor, served on county equalization board, been a member of the school board and at present is president of the village.

MARSH FAMILY

Deacon James Marsh came to Bridgewater from New Hartford, Conn., before 1800. Luke E. was born October 20, 1810. His son, William C. Marsh born December 11, 1848 married Elizabeth Bostwick. Their children are: Harry and Willard. Harry Luke (who is vice-president of the First National Bank of Crookston, Minn., married Annie Miller of Crookston, Minn. They have two children: Elizabeth Miller, aged 7 years, and Albert William, aged 1 year). Willard Bostwick is an instructor in Hamilton College.

BOSTWICK FAMILY

Levi Bostwick came to Bridgewater prior to 1800. He married Nancy Ives (a sister of Jesse Ives) who came from

Connecticut on horseback following a line of marked trees.   Mr. Bostwick built the present Hibbard House.   Levi Willard Bostwick was born in Bridgewater and spent his life in this town. He had two sons and one daughter: Charles Frederick Bostwick, John Mott Bostwick and Elizabeth Bostwick.   Elizabeth married Wm. C. Marsh and the two sons, Harry and Willard mentioned in the Marsh descendants are also the representatives of the Bostwick family.

PERKINS FAMILY

Allen M. Perkins came to Bridgewater in the year 1856. He had been engaged in the wholesale business in Utica, and opened a large general store on the corner where the Masonic Building and Rising's store is, including the whole corner.   A year later the entire corner was swept by fire, and he next engaged in business where the cottage hotel is now located, where he remained till 1870.   He then removed to Utica where he was engaged in business on South Street for some years.   Later he returned to Bridgewater where he spent his remaining years.

Mr. Perkins was a man of public spirit and was a leader in securing sidewalks for the village.   He was also the leading spirit of Methodism in the community and the Methodist church (the old Union church) was built largely through his enterprise and perseverance.

Mr. Perkins was born in Coventry, Conn., in 1813 and died in Bridgewater in 1895.   He was the son of a Baptist minister, Ransom Perkins.   He married Julia Robertson of Manchester, Conn.   Mrs. Perkins was born in 1809 and died in Bridgewater in 1896.   They had three children, Ransom, who enlisted in the Fifth New York Cavalry for the Civil War as a Corporal and was mustered out a Captain, died at Canton, Ill., in May, 1912, where he went after the war.   The two daughters are Jane L. Tompkins, widow of the late N. H. Tompkins of Whitesboro, and Antonette, wife of Charles W. Stoddard of Bridgewater. Their two children, Ralph and Florence, represent the early Perkins family as well as the Stoddard.

STODDARD FAMILY

Sherman Stoddard came to Bridgewater in the early

Forties. He was born in Madison, Madison County, March 25, 1819. In 1843 he married Julia Ann Teator of Bridgewater, who died October 7, 1901. Mr. Sotddard died April 12, 1902. He was a carpenter by trade. They had four children: Helen May, died in childhood; Julia Maria, born March 8, 1844, died November 17, 1897; Herbert, now resides in Flushing, Long Island; Theodore Henry, born December 19, 1852, and died November 8, 1913.

Charles W. Stoddard, the only survivor now living in Bridgewater, has been identified with the interests of the village all his life. He has had an intimate knowledge of men and affairs and his great memory has furnished us a lead to many of the important facts contained in this volume and has confirmed many others.

Charles married Antonette Perkins and their two children are Ralph and Florence.

PARKHURST FAMILY

Gould H. Parkhurst's ancestors on the paternal side came to America from England in 1659. There were three brothers who settled in Connecticut and Rhode Island, and of their posterity eleven took part in the Revolutionary War. Noah Parkhurst, who was the first to fire his musket at Concord Bridge, was his great uncle. Mr. Parkhurst's father, Gould T. Parkhurst, moved from Plainfield, Windham county, Connecticut, to the town of Winfield, Herkimer county, by wagon in 1809. His mother was of French Huguenot descent. Mr. Parkhurst received a good education and spent most of his life in the town of Bridgewater. At one time he was quite a prosperous farmer. He represented the town in the Board of Supervisors in 1875 and was elected Justice of the Peace in 1878, a position which he held for some time. In politics he was a Democrat and for several terms he filled the office of Justice of Sessions.

Gould T. Parkhurst and Hannah Healy were married April 20, 1809 and came from Connecticut that year and settled in Chepachet, town of Winfield. Gould H. was born March 27th, 1820. From Winfield they moved to Herkimer and there kept hotel and about 1830–1840 they came to Babcock Hill and conducted the hotel in what is now the Lemuel Tripp house. After this they moved to North Bridgewater and conducted the North Bridgewater hotel up to about 1853. On March 15, 1849, Gould H. Parkhurst married Hannah M. Brockway, to whom were born five children: Albert H., Charles M., Clara L., Katie Belle, and Helen M. Hannah M., wife of Gould H. Parkhurst, died February 17th, 1878. Mr. Parkhurst died June 4th, 1897. He gave all his children a good education and one son, who graduated from Hamilton College, died in Duluth. Of five children but one survives, Albert H. of North Bridgewater, with whom the father spent the closing years of his life. Justice Parkhurst was a man of high character and greatly esteemed by all who knew him. On other pages are found his sketches of the early life and activities of Bridgewater and much credit is due him for his painstaking efforts in preserving these records.

FOOTE FAMILY

Epaphroditus Foote married Annie Goodwin, the widow of Joel Ives, for his fourth wife. Their five children were Sophie, Joel, Emeline, Leonard, Rufus. Sophie married a Hall and one son, Joel, was born to them. Joel died at six years of age. Emeline married an Inglehart and they had three children, Hiram, Rufus and Sophie. Leonard married Hannah Clark and their three children were Mary (Dickson), George and Frederick. Rufus married Emily Hall and one son, William, was born. George Foote had one daughter, Anna, who married Earl Rising and they have one daughter, Gladys. Josephine Foote was the only daughter of William Foote and she married William Rowland and they have one daughter, Ethel.

CRANDALL FAMILY

Peter B. Crandall was one of the prominent men of the town of Bridgewater. He was born July 1, 1816 and was educated in Bridgewater and Cazenovia Seminary. For a time he taught school. He married Eunice Carter Priest in 1844. They built the P. B. Crandall house which is now standing on East street and was built in 1852 and 1853. For some years they ran their farm most successfully, but Mr. Crandall was often sought for in public office and was school commissioner for two terms. He was Captain and Provost-Marshal of the

21st District in 1865. They had four children which were born in Bridgewater at their farm home. Kirk Peter was born in 1846 and died April 5, 1910. He was a civil engineer, being educated at Hamilton College. He was city engineer for many years of Ithaca. He was an extensive traveler and graduated in 1869 from Hamilton College.

Charles Lee Crandall born in 1850. He attended school at West Winfield, Whitestown Seminary and graduated from Cornell University in 1872. Since that time he has been Professor of Railroad Engineering in the University.

Lucy Ella Crandall was born in 1853, was educated at Cornell. She married a Brazilian, Pedro de Mello, in 1879. Since time she has made her home in Brazil.

Clayton L. Crandall was born in 1858. He, too, graduated from Cornell and spent his life in Ithaca. He is a fruit and vegetable gardner.

Peter B. Crandall and family moved to Ithaca in the spring of 1868. Mr. P. B. Crandall was Supervisor of the town two terms.

WOODWORTH FAMILY

The first mention of the name of Woodworth in this country is found in the records of the town of Scituate, Mass. There has been no discovery of a Woodworth in any of the early settlements of this country prior to Walter Woodworth of Scituate. He came from Kent, England, about 1628.

Samuel Woodworth was a direct descendant from Walter Woodworth in the fourth generation, and was the earliest settler of the Woodworth family in Bridgewater. He was born in Norwich, Conn., June 25, 1771, was married June 12, 1790, moved to Columbia, Herkimer County in 1794 and to Bridgewater about 1813.

He was elected a member of Assembly in 1825. He died October 10, 1830.

Isaac Woodworth was the eldest son of Samuel Woodworth and was born in Bosworth, Conn., April 13, 1791. He came to Columbia, Herkimer County, with his father, Samuel, in 1794, and remained there until about 1821 when he removed to Bridgewater. Isaac and his father carried on a general merchandise store, bought and packed pork and cheese, and other country produce for shipment, when the only transportation facilities to and from Albany were with wagons.

He was a soldier in the War of 1812, and was quartermaster at Sacketts Harbor. He was appointed by Governor Daniel D. Tompkins justice of the Peace before he was 21 years old. He was twice married and was the father of eleven children, Augusta, Samuel, Wallace, Elvira, Ephraim, Chauncey, Granville, Harriet, Kate, Caroline and Charles.

Isaac Woodworth died in Rochester, Minn., May 11, 1870. His remains were brought to Bridgewater and buried in Fairview Cemetery.

Charles DeWolf, the youngest child of Isaac Woodworth, was born in Bridgewater, December 7, 1840, and has lived in this town all his life except for 13 years which he spent in the adjoining town of Brookfield. He has served in the capacity of Supervisor and Postmaster, and has always been interested in whatever has been for the best interests of the town or village. He was married October 25, 1869, to Kate Langworthy, and has no children. He is now hale and hearty and the last of the Woodworths in this vicinity.

BROWN FAMILY

Eleazer Brown came from Stonington, Connecticut, to Brookfield in 1774. He married Edith Palmer. Their children were: A. W. Brown, Prentice Brown. Prentice Brown was a blacksmith by trade and built the old blacksmith shop that was used by ''Broker Jones'' and stood by the little brook by East Street. He also built the two houses standing next to it, the one in which George Tripp lives and also the Claude Wilkinson house. He was off on the west hills burning a coal pit to make charcoal to use in the blacksmith shop, as soft coal was not known then, and he heard the sound of firing, etc. When he told his friends they laughed but it was learned later that there was a battle at Sacket's Harbor and he did really hear the cannons. He moved from Bridgewater to Hackley Street. Prentice Brown had two children, William Leroy, who married M. Angeline Wood; William Henry who married Hannah Penny and Alonzo Brown, who married Lizzie W. Dorland.

William Henry Brown has four children: Dr. Charles Brown, (whose children are Alfred and Elinor) Myron, May and Grace. Alonzo Brown has three children: Walter M. and their one child is named Ella A.; Claude E. married Lillian Wing and their son's name is Russell W.; William D. married Florence E. Howard and their son's name is Howard D.

SKETCHES

TWO REVOLUTIONARY MAJORS

Among the early settlers of the town were two men who distinguished themselves in American Revolution: Major Anthony Rhodes and Major Lorin Robbins, both natives of Connecticut. The former was the father of Squire Avery Rhodes, a prominent farmer and citizen of the town and grandfather of Judge A. L. Rhodes, an account of whose career is given on another page. The remains of Major Rhodes lie on the farm where he lived at Babcock Hill. He died in his 84th year. Major Lorin Robbins was held in high esteem by his neighbors. He left a family of ten sons and two daughters. One daughter became the wife of Martin Babcock; the other the wife of James Avery Rhodes. A tomb stone, bearing his name, stands in Fair View Cemetery. He did in his 89th year.

WILLIAM CROFT RUGER

William Croft Ruger was born in Bridgewater in 1824, the son of John Ruger, one of the prominent lawyers in the early history of the town. We get a glimpse of the nature of 'Squire Ruger by a story told by Dr. H. P. Whitford to the effect that Ruger was called upon by a resident of Madison county to defend him in some litigation. The lawyer was very conscientious, and his acceptance of a case was often based upon the amount of moral force revealed in his client in relating his side of the case, or in telling his story. In this particular case 'Squire Ruger was particularly moved over the injustice done his client, according to his own story, and asked him if he was certain that facts were as he had related them to him. His client affirmed that they were. "All right," said Mr. Ruger, "you go back and join issue and when the case is ready for trial

I will appear.'' He thoroughly prepared his case, and appeared on the day stated for his client. As the complainant was sworn, he objected to a line of questioning, and held the witness on the stand all morning without answering a question, and the case got no farther as the plaintiff gave it up in disgust, and withdrew his suit.

His son, William Croft, inherited the mind and powers of his father and rising in the legal profession step by step he was appointed in 1882 to the chair of Chief Justice of the Court of Appeals. On his death in 1892 Governor Roswell P. Flower in his Special Message to the Assembly gives the following high tribute to his name and career, which furnishes a splendid sketch of one of Bridgewater's honored sons:

''It is my sad duty to announce to the Legislature the death on Thursday last at his home in Syracuse of William C. Ruger, the Chief Judge of the Court of Appeals. So short was the period of his illness that the news of his death came with shock to the people of the state and the sense of public loss in his departure is general and profound.

''He gave the ripest years of his life to the service of the state. Born in 1824, thoroughly schooled by an active and successful practice of thirty-seven years in the law he was elected in 1882 at the age of fifty-eight to the highest judicial office within the gift of the state. In that distinguished office he fitly rounded out the period of a well spent life and splendidly supplemented as a judge the well-earned fame which had previously made him one of the foremost lawyers at the bar. His knowledge of the law, the rugged honesty of his convictions, his dignity, independence and great ability gave him universal respect among lawyers, as among the people. His judicial opinions have been substantial contributions to our jurisprudence, and the fearlessness which often accompanied their deliverance always challenged general admiration.

''His character was that of the best type of judge, steadfastly upright in private life, clear in his convictions of justice and tenacious in their defense, never swayed by popular clamor from his own conception of duty. The unusual distinction which he attained was the just recognition of distinguished abilities and the earnest purpose and his public career has won for him an enviable place in the history of the state.

"At this time of the people's mourning, which has ceased not with the dead jurist's burial, it is fitting that the Legislature should manifest in appropriate manner their recognition of Judge Ruger's eminent public services. I, therefore, recommend such action on the part of your honorable body as may fittingly record the esteem and respect in which he was held by the people and express in generous degree the widespread feeling of appreciation of his earnest fidelity to a great public trust.

"ROSWELL P. FLOWER."

AUGUSTUS L. RHODES

Bridgewater is proud to claim among her honored men the noted judge who rose to the high ranks in the legal and political world. In commemoration of this 91st birthday the San Jose (California) Mercury dated May 25, 1911, paid him a high tribute and parts of the article are quoted below to convey in a small way the love and esteem in which he has ever been held:

"A. L. Rhodes, pioneer jurist of Santa Clara county, honored and beloved by all who know him today celebrates with neither pomp nor ceremony his 91st birthday. Yesterday he completed the 90th round in life's fateful course and despite the weight of four score and ten years, he is still as active, virile and energetic in body and mind as ever. Tall, spare, commanding Father Time has shown great kindness to the aged jurist in the gentle tracery of gray with which his fleeting fingers have touched with honor the brow that has so nobly won its honors. None the less the astute Judge, he was also none the less gracious, cultured and kind gentleman as he accorded to The Mercury the exceptional privilege of recording a brief sketch of the life of one of the most exceptional men who have ever graced the bench of California, for Judge Rhodes came to the Golden State when his history was still in the embryotic making. That he has contributed much to her glory as a State that he has loved these many years, with the ardency of youth, the section which he has so long made his home; that he still looks upon her future with wonderful clairvoyance and a precision of reasoning power which even relentless age cannot obscure in any haze of failing faculties, may be seen from the clear, precise and concise statements which follow in almost the exact language of the narrator in the recital of a few of the guiding incidents of a long and virtuous history.

"This faculty of sane reasoning and omnipresent mental poise is, according to Judge Rhodes, merely a trait in his family tree, for his father, who died at the old homestead when he has attained almost the age of 96 and his grandfather and grandmother, who respectively attained ages near that figure, retained all their highest reasoning powers to the very last.

"The Mercury has no small pleasure in today presenting to its readers some of the sidelights of that splendid life not yet fully run—that life which may be readily counted as one of the foremost in California's galaxy of eminent men and learned jurists, for Judge Rhodes' opinions and rulings bear the rare distinction of having seldom been reversed by a court of higher appeal.

"Quiet, retiring, loving little ostentations, seeking not notoriety, it was difficult to make Judge Rhodes realize that the public has interest in his personality and his public life; but touching the chord of reminiscence with gentle hands he relaxed and told modestly of some of the episodes of his life which has made indelible impress upon his memory and in which he believed the public might find interest.

" 'I was born on the 25th of May, 1821 in the town of Bridgewater, Oneida County, N. Y. In that county I attended the common schools and academies having commenced the study of Latin when I was 11 years of age and so continued until I entered Hamilton College in that county in 1837. I graduated with the same class in which I entered in 1841. I received the degree of LL.D. from this college in 1870. After graduation I passed three or four years in Virginia, Florida and Georgia and then emigrated to Indiana in 1846. In that year I was admitted to the bar, after having studied the textbooks of the law without the aid of law office, teacher or law school. I immediately entered into practice of my profession in Green County, Ind., and continued until 1854, having been elected to one term as

District Attorney of the county.   In that year, 1854, my family and myself with a company of friends crossed the plains with teams, I steering for Santa Clara County, Cal., where I soon got a home and have since lived.'

"(Continuing with easy grace and ready flow of language, simply yet exquisitely expressed and deliberately uttered in clear, resonant tones, the Judge told in fascinating fashion of his judicial career in the new El Dorado, the land of promise, which had lured so many bold, brave men from the East to the setting sun.)

"'My health having been impaired by the malaria in Indiana, I supplemented the trip across the plains by living on a farm for a couple of years and in '56 I came into the town of San Jose, began the practice of law and continued in practice until I was elected in 1863 as one of the Justices of the Supreme Court.   Prior to that time I had been District Attorney of this county of Santa Clara and for one term of two years was State Senator, representing the counties of Alameda and Santa Clara.

"'My career upon the bench of the Supreme Court commenced in January, 1864, having been elected as I have just stated in 1863 at the same time with Judges Sanderson, Curry, Sawyer, and Shafter.   Upon the alloting of the terms of the Judges who were first elected, I was a candidate for re-election and was re-elected the further term of 12 years.   The Constitution which was adopted in 1879 cut off four years of that term and left my term really eight years, making 16 years altogether upon the bench of the Supreme Court.   After the expiration of my term of office I entered into the practice of my profession in San Francisco and so continued until I was appointed by Governor Gage in 1899 as Superior Judge to succeed Judge Kittredge recently deceased.   I remained as such Judge, discharging the duties of that office up to the time of resignation, the time of which I am not precisely sure, but I think it must have been three years ago.'

"While Judge Rhodes has achieved much in the affairs of men being in addition to his legal distinction a Regent of the University of California for eight years, he has achieved yet more in the love and esteem of his family, daughter and granddaughter, ministering with affectionate care and pardonable pride to their distinguished parent in his declining years, his wedded companion in life having already been called from his side.''

STEPHEN MOULTON BABCOCK

Stephen Moulton Babcock was born in the town of Bridgewater October 22d, 1843. He was the son of Peleg Brown and Cornelia Scott Babcock. His father was a prosperous farmer and was held in high esteem by his townsman, having been supervisor and at the time of his death, April 2d, 1857, a member of the New York State Legislature. It was the wish of his father that he should have a college education and with that in view he spent a term or two in the West Winfield Academy and finished his preparatory studies in Clinton Liberal Institute and in the fall following, entered Tufts College, from which he graduated four years later. His education up to this time had been along general lines and not specific. He turned his attention to chemistry, spending a short time in Cornell University and later taking a two years' course in the University of Gottingen, Germany, from which he received the degree of Ph.D. Later Tuft's College conferred the degree of LL.D. The Geneva Experimental Station, in looking for a chemist chose Dr. Babcock, which position he acceptably filled for a number of years. His services in connection with the station attracted the attention of the Wisconsin Agricultural College and the position of chemist was tendered him with an increased salary. A member of the Board of Control of the Geneva Experimental Station said, ''I shall miss the hearty laugh of the Doctor when I visit the station and I consider it a shame that the great state of New York could not retain the services of such a distinguished chemist.'' It might be well here to state that the Doctor thought the change would give him an added field of usefulness, which was afterward demonstrated by the invention of the Babcock Milk Test.

The State of Wisconsin through its Governor and Legislature in recognition of his services presented him with the largest bronze medal ever struck in England. The Test has done more to place dairying on a standard scientific basis than any other thing that has happened to it since man first began to squeeze milk out of the cow. Taking the world through among dairymen and distributors of milk the name of Babcock is a more familiar public word than Edison, Morse, Darwin or Whitney, all of whom are said to have changed history and thought. The perfection of this Test should be emphasized. It has never been improved. Without doubt Dr. Babcock could have patented his discovery and could it have been handled as other great discoveries have been, the people would have paid him high tribute until today he would have been classed with the world's millionaires. Instead of this he has given this discovery to the world and in doing this he did a greater thing for humanity than when he perfected the test.

He is still interested in the University that he has honored and honored him. He is greatly interested in his old home. He married in 1895 May Cornelia Crandall of Winfield. They are occasional visitors here and from their many friends receive a most hearty welcome.

DR. HIRAM PASCO WHITFORD

Hiram Pasco Whitford was born in Canterbury, Conn., in 1826. His father, William M. Whitford, was born on the same farm as Hiram Pasco. His mother's maiden name was Lucetta Tillinghast. They moved to Schuyler, Herkimer County, N. Y., in 1830 and to Bridgewater, Oneida County, in March 1842. Hiram read medical books at home from the age of 12 to 16. In 1850 he married Melissa Harrington. She died ten years later. Two children were born, a son and a daughter, both of whom graduated in medicine at the Eclectic Medical College in Cincinnati, where their father graduated in 1860. The son, Elwin Pasco is now, 1914, practicing with his father in Bridgewater. Previous to entering the Eclectic College in Cincinnati, Dr. Hiram P. Whitford read medicine two years with Dr. Van Vleck, a German physician in Hamilton, N. Y., after which he took the burden of the home farm from his father's shoulders for three years and entered college in 1859. Immediately after graduating in 1860 he began practicing in Bridgewater, where

DR. HIRAM PASCO WHITFORD

HERBERT E. PALMER

he still is. In 1868 Dr. Whitford was given up to die with tuberculosis. But he simply would not die and set out to find a way to prevent it. On the theory that tuberculosis structure is composed of cells lacking in necessary elements he set out by a strict hygiene and an extra nutritious diet to build up these cells anew. He succeeded and after fifty years of the strenuous life of a country doctor is still enjoying life at 88 years of age.

EMERSON M. WILLIS

Emerson M. Willis, who served with high credit as district attorney and is now in the active practice of law at Utica, was born at Columbia, Herkimer County, New York, February 27, 1874, a son of Marcus D. and Mary J. (McCormack) Willis. The Willis family came to America from England and Jane Lewis, the maternal grandmother, was a native of Wales. The grandparents on the paternal side were born in New York State. Grandfather John McCormack was in Virignia at the opening of the Civil War and was given thirty minutes in which to join the Confederacy or leave the community in which he was living, also leaving his property behind him. He came north and enlisted in the Union army in which he continued until the close of the war. He was captured and was for a time confined in a Confederate prison. After the expiration of his service he located at Waterville, New York, never returning to the south to reclaim his property. The father of our subject engaged in farming and for about thirty years past has made his home at Bridgewater.

Emerson M. Willis was reared on a farm and received his preliminary education in the country schools. Having decided upon a professional career, he matriculated in the law department of Union University at Albany and was graduated with the degree of LL.B. in 1894. He then entered the office of Josiah Perry of Utica and in 1897 was admitted to the bar. He remained with Mr. Perry until 1898 when he was appointed attorney for the sheriff's office, which position he held for nearly a year, but resigned to accept an appointment as assistant district attorney. He served in this capacity through two

administrations and attracted such favorable attention that he
was elected district attorney and assumed office January 1,
1905, being re-elected in 1907.   During his period of office he
disposed of a number of important cases among which were the
graft cases which ended in the imprisonment of several persons.
Another case of unusual interest was that known as the Gulf
Murder Mystery.   Mr. Willis succeeded in ferreting out the
guilty man and sending him to the electric chair.   While in
office Mr. Willis was especially noted for economy in administration and expeditious trial of cases, two factors of great importance to taxpayers and to all who are interested in the effective administration of public affairs.   On the 1st of January, 1905, Mr. Willis associated with J. DePeyster Lynch in the
practice of law under the title of Lynch & Willis, now one of
the leading law firms of Utica.   Mr. Willis has had two recent
calls from the people of Oneida County to serve in public office.
The first request was that he should become a candidate for
justice of the supreme court in 1909, while the other urged him
to allow his name to be used as a candidate for congress in 1910.
The petition in the latter instance was signed by more than
three thousand voters.   He was a candidate in 1901 before
the convention in the Fifth Judicial District for justice of the
supreme court and had the unanimous support of Oneida and
Herkimer Counties, but owing to the fact that Oswego County
was not represented on the bench the nomination was given to
that county.   Since he has respectfully resisted all efforts urg-
ing him to re-enter public life.   He is interested in a number of
important cases now pending in the courts and possessing
marked natural ability and a wide knowledge of law, is one of
the leaders of the Oneida County bar.

On the 28th of June, 1899, Mr. Willis was united in marriage to Miss Julia E. Penney, a daughter of Giles A. Penney,
of Unadilla Forks.   Two children have blessed this union:
John D., who was born April 20, 1901, and Marjorie E., born
March 28, 1906.   Mr. Willis is a stanch adherent of the Republican party and is regarded as one of the most effective cam-
paign speakers appearing upon the platform in this part of the
state.   He is clear and forcible in his utterance and has few
superiors in carrying an argument to a logical conclusion.   He.

is safe counselor and as a lawyer ranks with the best at the Oneida County bar. He has a host of friends who place implicit confidence in his judgment and integrity and prophesy for him a brilliant and highly successful future whether in public life or as a practitioner of law.

THREE SCHOOL PRINCIPALS

(Subjects of Illustrations)

Three men who have made an impress at different periods on Bridgewater schools are Professors L. D. Browne, John Bayly Swinney and Earle Stanley Lougee.

Prof. L. D. Browne, the first principal of the Union School was educated in the select schools of Jordanville and at West Winfield Academy and Whitestown Seminary and began teaching at the age of seventeen. He first became principal of the Mohawk Graded School and Whitestown Union school. He also taught Newport High School ten years and two years a select school in Newport. He spent two years in Bridgewater Union School and for several years his pupils of that day have held a reunion each year. Miss Mary Murphy was the first Assistant at Bridgewater and she has since passed away. Since leaving Bridgewater, Mr. Browne has been associated with the New York Life Insurance Company of New York.

Prof. John Bayly Swinney, the first principal of the High School, to whom great credit is due for the excellent work accomplished during his management, came to Bridgewater from Syracuse University. After his work in Bridgewater he was superintendent of Schools in Springville, N. Y., for a term of two years. Soon after this he was employed at Wanamaker's, New York, and at a later period was with the publishing house of Longman, Green & Company. Since this time he has been on the editorial staff of the Alexander Hamilton Institute of New York City.

Prof. Earle Stanley Lougee, A. B., the present principal of the Union School, is a graduate of Syracuse University, Class of 1912. After graduating from there he was with Dodd, Mead & Company of New York for a short time and came to Bridgewater in December, 1912, where he has done excellent work in the upbuilding of the school.

L. D. BROWNE
Principal of Bridgewater Union
School, 1882

EARLE STANLEY LOUGEE
Principal of Bridgewater School

JOHN BAYLY SWINNEY
Principal of Bridgewater High School
1902

FACTS AND OCCURRENCES

THE MONROE TAVERN.

Abraham Monroe was an early settler and kept a public house on the place owned in later years by John Tuckerman, now in possession of the Tuckerman family.

This house is considerably over 100 years old, and was known as the Monroe Tavern, and continued as such until about 1854. Regarding this historic house, Miss Bertha Tuckerman, the daughter of John Tuckerman, gives these few historic lines:

"It had a large ball room, and my grandmother, Julia Ives, came here to a dance before she was married. The old fire-places and arched ceiling of the ball-room are preserved, though it has been made into a hall and two sleeping rooms. We have several articles of use in the household belonging to my grand-father and grandmother—a chair, a bureau, salver, cup and saucer, teapot, etc.''

A CENTENARIAN

November 4th, 1909, there began a three days' celebration in her home of the 100th birthday of Mrs. Maria Brown Robin-son. Maria Brown was the eighth child of Asa and Lucy Dow Brown, pioneer settlers in the hills of Brookfield. Their father served in the Revolution. When she was nine years old they moved to a farm in Richfield. She came here in girlhood to attend the Academy, living with her sister, Mrs. Phiny Brewer or her uncle, Judge Oliver Brown, later and for many years partner with her brother, Benj. Brown, in the store at Unadilla Forks.

She united with the Baptist church in Richfield in her sixteenth year, was a member of that church until her death, Jan 15, 1910, an unusual record of membership and the longest one known in that denomination. March 22, 1838 she married Joseph Robinson, from Kimbolton, England. They lived on a farm in Richfield. She was a true helpmeet of those days, pre-paring the wool and flax, spinning and weaving and making the family clothing and household goods and doing all the household work, caring for and training the six sons and one daughter, always interested in whatever was for the good of her country or the community in which she lived and there is still a tradition of how she always found time to help a sick neighbor.

In 1872, leaving two of their sons on the farm, they moved to "Rest Knoll," their home in the village of Richfield, where her doors swung with hospitable welcome. This was the 59th anniversary of their marriage, Joseph Robinson dying on March 22, 1897.

Their daughter, Lucy M. Robinson, came from Minnesota to make glad her mother's last years. In her 90th year they took a three month's pleasure trip to Minnesota. February 22, 1900, the home was destroyed by fire. They then purchased the house so long owned by David Wood and made their home in the village of her schooldays. She was a woman of great mental poise and physical energy, capable and helpful in every department of life, even in her last years retaining her wisdom and good judgment.

She recovered from many severe sicknesses. In her 98th year for a long time unable to even move in bed—when she rallied with mind still strong she determined she would not be bed-ridden. With wonderful will power she regained the use of her limbs. Only those with her can realize how hard it was to revive those aged muscles to use again, but strong determination did it and she was about the house until the day she died, often walking to some neighbor's. She had always been a great reader and kept in touch with the times, reading the daily papers until the very last. Many who came to know her said they should always be so glad for they would no longer dread growing old themselves.

The Sunday before Mrs. Robinson's centennial birthday was celebrated as Old Folks' Sunday in the Congregational church here, and she walked up to the front of the pulpit and in a strong, clear voice heard by everyone in the crowded church, she led the responsive reading. Every guest at her centennial celebration was presented a candle which they lighted from the tall one from the table where she presided, just as the light of her life, ever strong in its purpose, will shine on and on through all who knew her.

"BEAR HUNTING"

During the early settlement of the town an eight-year-old son of Ephraim Waldo was out playing in the woods one day when he discovered a young bear asleep by a log. This lad had inherited the adventurous spirit of the pioneer and being anxious to capture the prize the noislessly proceeded to an elm tree at a short distance, peeled off a piece of bark, and returned to the peaceful slumberer. Making a noose in the improvised lasso, he proceeded cautiously to the opposite side of the log and reaching over succeeded in fastening the cord around little "Bruin's" neck. He was a true backwoodsman and he knew that the old bear would be within close hearing distance and he accordingly tightened the noose to prevent his captive from uttering a cry. Having performed this feat he attempted to lead his captured prize home but found that he was very averse of being broken to a halter, but the lad persevered and had come upon the highway when Mother Bruin followed in close pursuit to reclaim her wanderer. Jesse Ives luckily happened to discover the trio and getting his gun quickly disposed of the old bear and the lad reached home safely with his trophy.

BILL OF SALE

The following interesting document has been preserved by L. R. Scott in its original form. It is written on heavy parchment, much discolored and creased by age and has the appearance of being charred. It has the old-time blood seal attached to witness and much of the writing is difficult to decipher but by close and persistent study the entire bill has been interpreted and brings to our attention the days of slavery in Bridgewater.

KNOW ALL MEN by these presents That I, Peter Smith, of Utica, County of Oneida and State of New York, for and in consideration of Three Hundred and fifty Dollars to me in hand paid, at and before the sealing and delivery of these presents by Jesse Ives of Whitestown, County and State aforesaid, have bargained for and delivered and do by these presents bargain, sell and herewith deliver unto the said Jesse Ives, his Heirs and Assigns, three negro slaves, viz: One Negro Woman, named Diane, her male child about six years old, her female child about three years old, and also another female child said to be born free, agreeable to law, about eighteen months old.

As witness my hand and seal at Utica, August 17th, eighteen hundred and one.

NOTE—Between eleventh and twelfth lines the words "named Diane" were interlined before signed.

PETER SMITH.

WITNESS: Jerahmeel Ballou.

"EXTRACT FROM A LETTER"

The following excerpt was taken from a letter by J. M. Trowbridge, written to the "Silver Leaf," a small paper published in Bridgewater at the time. Mr. Trowbridge was a former physician of the town and lived in the W. C. Marsh house. It refers to the elm trees that border the walk and points out the age and growth of these lofty "sentinels."

Brooklyn, N. Y., February 14, 1894.

Publishers of the Silver Leaf:

The row of elms in front of our old homestead, as well as many other trees through the village were planted under the charter. The trees were planted as early as 1829 or 1830. * * * Our homestead by the big cherry tree was built in 1822 or 1823. I was born in that house in April, 1824. My brother Aobert, three years older, was born in the frame building standing on the south side of the turnpike a few feet west of the brick store building on the southwest corner of the crossing of the turnpike and the north and south road. It was known, I think, as the old Stoddard tavern Stand. These dates fix the age of the homestead building very closely. I think it dates from 1830. The row of elms were so young in 1831 or 1832 that I, a boy of seven or eight, bent one of them to the ground and was badly scared for doing so by Tom Allen, son of Stephen Allen, who told me I would be put in jail for it. * * *

Very truly yours,

J. M. TROWBRIDGE.

RAILROADS

D., L. & W. RAILROAD

Bridgewater has two railroads, the Richfield Branch of the Delaware, Lackawanna and Western and the Unadilla Valley. The former connects with the Utica Division of the Lackawanna at Richfield Junction and runs to Richfield Springs.

The road was built from Richfield Junction to West Winfield in 1869, as the Utica and Unadilla Valley Railroad. In 1870 it was leased by the Lackawanna, which corporation had acquired the portion running from Utica to Sherburne, under a lease for ninety-nine years, under which term the Company guaranteed the stockholders six per cent. interest. The following year, 1870, the Lackawanna continued the road to Richfield Springs.

The office was opened in Bridgewater in 1869, a Mr. Gallup, an expert in railroad business being in charge, and instructing Newton Sholes, the first agent. Charles W. Stoddard was clerk under Clark M. Barden, when the office was opened. The paint in the station was not dry and the first day's business had to be done in a box car. Later George E. Woodman became passenger ticket agent and Mr. Stoddard was freight agent.

When the road was built the question of getting over the hill from the Sauquoit valley was an engineering problem. Some favored going over Paris Hill, but Civil Engineer Hunt said, "This road will be built for all time, and we may as well take the shortest way, and it will be no more expensive."

H. C. Miller is the present agent of the two railroads.

UNADILLA VALLEY RAILROAD

This line connects with the Richfield Branch of the Lackawanna at Bridgewater, and the New Berlin Branch of the Ontario & Western Railroad at New Berlin. It was opened at New Berlin, at which were present business men from Utica and other large commercial centers.

The work was begun in 1889, and the honor of turning the first spade of earth, fell to the late N. N. Peirce of Bridgewater, whose interest in the project had been such as to promote general confidence in it in this section. Through a gentleman connected with the Babcock Company of Leonardsville Albert C. Couch of New York City, a professional promoter was interested. The road passed through the various vicissitudes of all enterprises of the kind, and after reaching Leonardsville from New Berlin, work was held up several years. Finally it was built to Bridgewater in 1894 through the efforts of D. C. Vulver of New York. Sufficient capital to pay all the claims was lacking and it was sold at auction to Dr. L. R. Morris of New York City, the present owner.

The first survey would have carried the road through the village right through the center of the Porter house and in the rear of the Penney residence, connecting with the Lackawanna near Herbert Palmer's barn. The right of way was too expensive for the promoters, and at the suggestion of a citizen of Bridgewater the survey for the present roadbed was made which right of way did not cost over $800. The other would have exceeded $10,000.

The present officers are: Wirt Howe, General Manager, New York; R. D. Perkins, Superintendent, New Berlin; H. A. Brome, General Freight and Passenger Agent, New Berlin.

LINE OF PROPERTY

The original boundary lines known as "The Line of Property" touched the head streams of the Unadilla where they rise in the north-western part of Bridgewater. The history of this original boundary line is full of interest to those not familiar with the term. For a great many years the absence of a fixed boundary line between the Six Nations and their dependencies on the one side and the Colonies of Pennsylvania, Maryland, Virginia, New Jersey and New York on the other was the subject of much controversy and contention. The outcome of this was the constant complaints from the Indians and encroachments from the whites and at every yearly meeting that the Indians held with the Governor at Albany this was the subject of a great share of their negotiations. A remedy had to be found and on Nov. 5, 1768, a convention was held at Fort Stanwix at which were present representatives from the colonies and from the Indian nations. A boundary line was settled and was as follows—It began at the mouth of the Tennessee (then Cherokee or Hohohege) River, near the junction of the Ohio with the Mississippi, up along the south banks of the Ohio to Killamy, above Fort Pitt (now Pittsburg), to the west branch of the Susquehanna, across the Alleghany mountains to the east branch of the Susquehanna and up that branch to the Oswego river, then to the Delaware river and up the Delaware to a point opposite where the Tianaderha (The Unadilla) empties into the Susquehanna, then across to the west branch of the Unadilla and up this river to its head, then in a straight line to the junction of Canada Creek with Wood Creek at the west of the carrying place beyond Fort Stanwix. This was the "Line of Property" but that part of it from the head of the Unadilla in Bridgewater to Wood Creek is more generally known by that term than any of the other portions. Soon after this boundary was made the Patent of Coxeborough was granted which extended the entire length of this part of the line and was bounded by it on the west. The tracts granted to this state by the Oneidas after the Revolution were bounded on the east by this "Line of Property" and this term has been used in subsequent conveyances and many have wondered of the origin and singularity of it, but knew little of its history. Just at the foot of College hill in the village of Clinton a stone may be seen which was erected by the Class of 1887 of Hamilton College to mark this "Line of Property."

GLEANINGS

Dr. Whitford built the first sidewalk in Bridgewater in 1864.

Miss Charlotte Ives had in her possession a gun which was used in the French war in 1755–60 and which also saw service during the Revolution. It was carried at the battle of Oriskany (August 6, 1777) by Miss Ives' great grandfather, the maternal grandfather of Jesse Ives. He was in that battle with his son and the latter fell over a stump or log and broke both his arms. This gun was also in use at the time of the burning of Danbury, Connecticut.

In the winter of 1801–2 the smallpox broke out and numbers were afflicted with it. By-laws were adopted by the town board for devising means wherewith to check its progress and care for those who were sick. In 1804 this town, in common with many others, suffered from the effects of a malarial fever, which carried to their graves many of the settlers.

Before the War Bridgewater was the center for a great many debates. The Fugitive Slave Law was especially discussed. For three nights in succession it was debated at the old Academy. They then went to the North church and the debate was continued three whole days in succession.

1843 was the last year for the annual General Training Day. Every able bodied man between 21 and 45 was served with a written notice to appear on a certain day armed and equipped according to law. The equipment was a gun, but if that was not available a stick would do. The day was spent in organizing and drilling. The whole family attended and most of them carried their dinner. The last Major General was O. B. Brown. A cannon was kept in the village in a house of its own for use on these occasions.

The last slave in Bridgewater was owned by Mr. Groves who lived in the Langworthy house. This slave was buried in the old cemetery back of the Congregational church. Most of the bodies were taken from this plot and moved to Fairview cemetery but it is claimed that the bones of this slave still rest there.

A story is told of a Mr. Platner who went to New York and purchased a slave and kept her for many years. Later becoming reduced financially he decided to sell her again and a deal was made with a lawyer and the human "chattel" was transferred. The lawyer soon afterward discovered the woman to be blind in one eye and he accordingly sued Platner and exacted from him nearly all his means.

CIVIC HISTORY

TOWN OF BRIDGEWATER

The town of Bridgewater has a population of 832 according to the census of 1910. It was formed from Sangerfield in 1797. Little of the early records are preserved that would throw light upon the intervening past. The following items are illuminating concerning the method of selecting town officers in that early day:

"Annual town-meeting opened in Bridgewater April 4, 1797. Agreeable to a law in that case made and provided, the freeholders and inhabitants (qualified to vote for town officers) met at the house of Colonel Thomas Converse in Bridgewater.

"Voted to choose town officers by ballot."

The following were the officers chosen, viz: Supervisor, Thomas Brown, Esq.; Town Clerk, Aaron Morse; Assessors, James Kinne, Esq., Eldad Corbit and William Morgan; Overseers of the Poor, Ezra Parker, John W. Brown and Alexander Tackles; Road Commissioners, Levi Carpenter, Jr., Job Tyler and James Benham, Jr.; Constable, John Mitchell; School Commissioners, Asher Flint, Thomas Brown, Esq., and Jonathan Porter; Collector, John Mitchell; Fence-Viewers, Ebenezer Barker, Joseph Moore and Abijah Babcock.

The following pathmasters were then chosen for the districts in the same order as they are named, from one to twelve: Zerah Brown, Ebenezer Barker, Jonathan Condy, Jesse Hall, Asher Bull, Asher Flint, Joseph Gardnier, Jonathan Utley, Jr., Stephen Gordon, Elijah Thompson, Truman Blackman and Jesse Carpenter.

The following have been Supervisors of Bridgewater since 1798:

1798–1800—James Kinne, Esq.	1814 —Samuel Jones, Jr.
1801–1802—Job Tyler	1815–1817—Willard Crafts
1803 —Asher Flint	1818 —Oliver Brown
1804–1806—Peabody Fitch	1819–1821—Samuel Jones
1807–1813—Daniel Rindge	1822 —Willard Crafts

1823	—Sardius Denslow
1824	—James A. Rhodes
1825–1826	—Sardius Denslow
1827	—Willard Crafts
1828	—Samuel Jones
1829	—Peleg Brown
1830–1831	—Absalom L. Groves
1832–1835	—Laurens Hull
1836	—Levi Carpenter
1837	—Peleg Brown
1838	—Theodore Page
1839	—John F. Trowbridge
1840	—James A. Rhodes
1841–1842	—Peleg Brown
1843–1844	—Oliver R. Babcock
1845	—Oliver B. Brown
1846	—Milton Converse
1847	—John Southworth
1848	—Everett Lewis
1849	—Samuel DeWolf
1850	—Elisha Baker
1851–1854	—Peleg B. Babcock
1855	—Nehemiah N. Peirce
1856	—Elisha B. Brown
1857	—William N. Southworth
1858–1860	—Peter B. Crandall
1861–1862	—Albert A. Steele
1863–1864	—Milton Converse
1865–1866	—J. Jerome Budlong
1867–1869	—Nehemiah N. Peirce
1870–1871	—Albert N. Bort
1872	—William Foote
1873–1874	—A. N. Bort
1875	—Gould H. Parkhurst
1875–1877	—Newton Sholes
1879–1880	—William N. Southworth
1881–1882	—Nehemiah N. Peirce
1883–1884	—George W. Palmer
1885	—Samuel Williams
1886–1887	—Davis S. Wood
1888	—George N. Greenman
1889–1890	—Robert Williams
1891	—Henry Robinson
1892	—Charles D. Woodworth
1893–1895	—Henry Sorn
1896–1898	—William Walsh
1898–1899	—Henry Sorn
1899–1901	—Robt. J. Williams
1901–1904	—Frank E. Rowe
1904–1905	—Herbert E. Palmer
1905–1909	—Roy Peirce
1909–1911	—Wm. Walsh
1911–1915	—William H. Rowland

THE VILLAGE

Bridgewater, like most rural communities without industries has suffered loss in population, owing to the centralization of industry and distribution of commodities. Its population now is 245. The village was incorporated in 1825, and was reincorporated in 1897 under the General Village Law. One of the first ordinances after the village was reincorporated designated the names of the various streets as follows:

Main Street—All that portion of the Utica and New Berlin Plank Road from the old Cherry Valley Turnpike north.

Unadilla Street—All that portion of the Utica and New Berlin Plank Road from the old Cherry Valley Turnpike south.

State Street—All that part of the old Cherry Valley Turnpike east of Main and Unadilla Street.

West State Street—All that part of the Cherry Valley Turnpike west of Main and Unadilla Streets.

Cottage Street—All that street from the D. L. & W. Railroad west to the head of the street formerly called the "Lane."

Pleasant Street—All that street from the D. L. & W. Railroad south to State street.

Beaver Street—All that street from Unadilla Street west.

BRIDGEWATER OF THE PRESENT

The civic organization is maintained in the simplest way, so as not to be a burden to the taxpayers. Yet the charter provides an easy method for the people of the village to make public improvements and levy taxes for the same when it is deemed necessary.

The disastrous fire in September, 1913, led the taxpayers to vote to purchase two chemical engines, and a fire company was organized. Like all rural villages the spirit to make "Country life" pleasant and comfortable with modern conveniences is taking hold of Bridgewater. The Trenton Falls Power Company is expected to extend its line through to West Winfield next Spring, and the village will take steps to provide street lighting and householders may avail themselves of the same.

In 1914 the new state road from Utica to Winfield was completed giving a macadam highway of superior construction for Main and State Streets. Its proximity to Utica, its natural attractions, and inviting natural beauty will unite to facilitate the development of Bridgewater as an attractive rural residential town. The spirit of enterprise is manifest among leading citizens who take pride in the old home town. Mr. Frederick P. Peirce of New York has always been interested in his native town, and other expatriated sons have an abiding interest here.

The President of the village is Mr. Herbert E. Palmer, who is safely and sanely progressive. Mr. Palmer has the confidence of the people, and possesses a fair conception of what improvements are needed and how to secure them at the least cost. The Trustees are in accord with him, and are anxious to make progress in developing the natural attractiveness of the village.

The following are the village officials: President, Herbert E. Palmer; Trustees, E. D. Montgomery, C. H. Clark; Clerk, H.

C. Miller; Treasurer, H. C. Rogers; Collector, L. H. Belz; Street Commissioner, Milton Tripp.

The Bridgewater Band is also an organization which deserves special mention. Music is advocated in the development of country life, and the small towns are developing their musicians. Bridgewater has a creditable organization.

BUSINESS PLACES

Today the general stores of Bridgewater are of recognized standing by the people of the village and surrounding community, carrying only lines of established quality. There are three of these: E. M. & H. O. Rising; Henry C. Rogers, in whose store the post office and the telephone exchange are located; and W. G. Roberts. Henry Sorn is postmaster. C. H. Clark is the feed and coal merchant, and is located in the old Lackawanna station. Amenzo Cole, R. J. Wilkinson and Michael Kehoe are the village blacksmiths. L. H. Belz is the tonsorial artist.

Bridgewater has two excellent hostelries, the Hibbard House, conducted by E. D. Montgomery, and the Cottage Hotel, conducted by Thomas Carney.

The community relies upon the natural resources of the farm, and this rich dairying section has a ready market for the product of "Bossy" in New York city. The Rider Milk station ships milk in bulk over the Lackawanna and the Phenix Milk station controlled by the Borden Condensed Milk Company ships over the Unadilla Valley and the Ontario and Western to New York.

INDEX

Babcock Hill 35
Babcock, Stephen Moulton 97
Baptist Church 55
Bear Hunting 105
Bill of Sale 105
Bridgewater 5
Bridgewater, 1830–1835 9
Bridgewater, of Present 114
Bridgewater, Village of 113
Buildings 73
Business Places 115
Centenarian, A 103
Church, Old Center 43
Churches 51
Civic History 112
Congregational Church 51
D., L. & W. Railroad 107
Descendants 77
Early Settlement 5
Episcopal Church 53
Fraternities 57
Geographical and Geological 5
Gleanings 110
Kismet Chapter, O. E. S. 60
Letter, Extract from a 106
Line of Property 109
Majors, Two Revolutionary 92
North Bridgewater 27
Pioneers 6
Principals, Three School 102
Railroads 107
Rhodes, Augustus L. 94
Ruger, William Croft 92
Schools 65
Settlement, Early 5
Settlers, Other (Bridgewater) 8
Settlers, Other (North Bridgewater) 30
Sketch, Historic 13
Sketches 92
Societies 57
Society of Friends 30
Stage Coach Days 69
Tavern, Monroe 103
Tavern, The Old 31
Town, Bridgewater 112
Unadilla Valley Grange 61
Unadilla Valley Railroad 107
Universalist Church 52
Various Industries 31